To Dick

Merry Christmas
from
Aunt Gertie
1940

EDGAR A. GUEST SAYS
It Can Be Done

EDGAR A. GUEST SAYS
It Can Be Done

THE REILLY & LEE CO.
Publishers   *Chicago*

IT COULDN'T BE DONE

Somebody said that it couldn't be done
  But he with a chuckle replied
That "maybe it couldn't," but he would be one
  Who wouldn't say so till he'd tried.
So he buckled right in with a trace of a grin
  On his face. If he worried he hid it.
He started to sing as he tackled the thing
  That couldn't be done, and he did it.

Somebody scoffed: "Oh, you'll never do that;
  At least no one ever has done it;"
But he took off his coat and he took off his hat,
  And the first thing we knew he'd begun it.
With a lift of his chin and a bit of a grin,
  Without any doubting or quiddit,
He started to sing as he tackled the thing
  That couldn't be done, and he did it.

There are thousands to tell you it cannot be done,
  There are thousands to prophesy failure;
There are thousands to point out to you one by one
  The dangers that wait to assail you.
But just buckle in with a bit of a grin,
  Just take off your coat and go to it;
Just start in to sing as you tackle the thing
  That "cannot be done," and you'll do it.

ACKNOWLEDGMENT

—of our appreciation to the persons who have graciously granted us permission to include in this book the interesting stories of their achievements is hereby extended to:

Mr. Milton H. Arndt	Mr. Douglas Leigh
Mr. Frank E. Austin	Mrs. Alice Foote MacDougall
Miss Emily P. Bissell	Mrs. Violette P. Payne
Mr. Leonard Burgweger	Mrs. Polly Pettit
Dr. George Washington Carver	Mr. John S. Redshaw
Sergeant Sidney Clay	Mrs. Jean O'Haver Shassere
Mr. Charles B. Darrow	Mr. A. G. Sherman
Mr. George K. End	Mr. David A. Smart
Captain Richard A. Fennelly	Mr. Thornton Snead
Mr. Lester Gaba	Mr. Walter M. Snead
Mr. Chester Gould	Mrs. Ora H. Snyder
Dr. John R. Gregg	Mrs. Cora Wilson Stewart
Mr. Mark G. Harris	(Mrs.) Ebba Sundstrom
Professor Leonarde Keeler	(Nylander)
Mr. Floyd Kinley	Mr. Egbert Van Alstyne
Mr. M. M. Kinley	Mr. Arthur B. Williamson
Mrs. Roy Largent	Mr. Robert C. Zuppke

CONTENTS

INTRODUCTION

Once a week Edgar A. Guest takes the train—always the same train—from Detroit to Chicago to read his poetry and act as host on the *It Can Be Done* radio program the following evening. Upon his arrival in Chicago he meets at his hotel the man in charge of his broadcast and together they select the poems that are to be read. Then down to the studio they go for the morning session of the grueling eight to ten hours of rehearsal—ten hours for a half hour on the air! During those hours every detail is hammered through to perfection, for every spoken word must accomplish over the air what sound and scenery and action combined do on the stage.

The chief production man who directs the show, with his stop watch in hand, marks off every minute on the script, in spite of the fact that the experienced writer who prepared it had already planned the timing with excruciating care. A few seconds must be taken off this speech and added to that for dramatic effect, one actor speaks more slowly than another, all these must be noted on the script so that there will not be the slightest degree of variation, for the program must fill the time to the dot—not a single word left over, not a second of blank time unused.

In addition to Mr. Guest, who is the star of the program, and a guest of honor whose life is the theme of it, a cast of from ten to sixteen actors and actresses, one announcer, one narrator, three production men, one engineer, three sound effects men—surrounded by everything from fire sirens to typewriters and telephone bells—a soloist and the orchestra, with its leader, are required for each broadcast. Every eye must be on the chief production man who, from the control room, a glass enclosed box above the stage, "irons out" the program and "gets it to jell." During rehearsal he talks to the actors through a microphone connected with the stage, but during the broadcast, of course, all instructions must be conveyed by motions—a finger to his nose means everything's running on time—*on th' nose.* A circular, winding-up movement of his hand, fast or moderate, says to speed up. To slow down a speech or scene he uses both hands in a motion of stretching something out. For "calm down" he uses the conventional downward motion of the hands, whereas a lifting movement calls on the actor at whom he is looking to "pep it up."

With him in the control room sits the engineer at a desk, beside what looks like a switchboard and in front of something not unlike a dashboard. He turns on and off microphones scattered around the stage, adjusts the public address system in the air theater and maintains balance between narration, music and sound effects. Through a loud speaker above their heads, the show comes to the production man and the engineer with exactly the same tone that goes out to the radio audience.

Thirty seconds before time to go on the air comes the cue and the production man holds his arms high above his head. The tense, expectant hush among actors and the audience in the small theater reaches top pitch. Twenty-five seconds pass. Then at a signal from the master control room, the production man abruptly points to the stage. The show starts. WE'RE ON THE AIR!

NIMBLE AND NUMB

If you are faced with a serious problem, if you think the world's against you, just consider the story of Arthur Williamson, who proved that the will to succeed can surmount any handicap. Pain, discouragement, despair—these were the somber notes that underscored his life; but over-borne by the ringing notes of his brave spirit, the sorrow and pain sink beneath the melody.

It was back in January, 1930, at Scottsdale, Pennsylvania, where is located the office of a tree-surgery company, that the tapestry of his life began—a tapestry as stirring as any—ancient or modern. Fifteen below zero stood the thermometer that blustery winter afternoon as Arthur Williamson, then only twenty years old, waited with his convertible coupe at the office of his employer, ready for his trying forty-five mile drive across the slopes to Pittsburgh with the company payroll.

"Fifteen below now, and getting colder," warned his friends, looking unenviously at the little car, "and getting colder. It's probably twenty out on the open road."

"Listen, fellows," answered Arthur gamely. "I'm not looking for any sympathy. My job is to drive this payroll to Pittsburgh, and I'm mighty thankful to have a job."

"Well, you better put on two pairs of mittens, pal," tossed in a friend. "Watch your fingers and ears!"

Little did light-hearted Arthur Williamson think then that this forty-five mile drive was to change the entire course of his life. He had a job to do, and he did it—gladly. Arriving in Pittsburgh, he discharged his duties and quickly began the lonely ride back to Scottsdale. But as he neared Greensburg, another car approached to within a short distance behind him. Within it were two grim-faced men, driving toward an ill-fated rendezvous.

"Gettin' close to the spot, Pete?" observed one, who was called Mike.

"Yea," answered Pete. "'Bout a half mile now."

"We'll pull up next to the kid and tell him to stop. He thinks we're cops. When he stops, Shorty crawls out of the rumble seat and bims him with that stocking full of mud. Then we finish him."

"And hit for New York with the dough. O.K. Sit tight. We're going to pass him at the next bend."

As the cars spun around the next icy curve, Mike challenged, "All right, you! Pull over to the side of the road. C'mon, pull over!"

"Who? Me?" answered Art Williamson. "I'm not speeding. I just—"

But he never finished the sentence, nor even the thought; for Shorty's blackjack knocked him cold—even for that twenty-below day.

"Nice work, Shorty," complimented Pete. "Give him another one, so he won't get up too quick. Me and Mike'll case his car. Then for New York. We ought to get plenty for workin' in weather like this."

Half an hour later, the biting wind of that bitter January night blew down upon a single, forlorn figure—the body of Arthur Williamson, abandoned by his assailants, stripped of his personal belongings, cruelly beaten . . . left to die. Then the indomitable spark of life that ignites the being of this brave youngster flickered feebly. Slowly, wearily, he staggered to his feet and, leaning into the wind, floundered his way toward a faint light in a farm house far away.

Hours later, it seemed to him, he was knocking at the door, feebly calling, "Open up. Open up, please. Help . . . help."

The farmer within flashed a spotlight on him and then complained to his wife, "Looks like a bum to me." To Arthur he said, "Can't do nothin' for you, stranger. Sorry. Can't take in drunks. Better try the foundry. It's only a thousand feet away. There's a fire there."

"Thousand feet," thought Arthur dimly in his submerged mind. "Fire . . . a few more feet." Indomitably he staggered onward. But he never made it!

They found him unconscious at eight o'clock the next morning, after he had been exposed to twenty-two below zero weather for six hours!

Three weeks later, in a hospital room, his mother pleaded with the doctor who was attending her boy. "But you don't understand, doctor, what his fingers mean to him . . . Arthur."

Very patiently the doctor explained, "Some of the toes have responded to treatment, but the fingers . . . "

"You mean?"

"Three toes must be amputated, and his fingers . . . "

"His fingers?"

"We can save one joint of each finger and his left thumb."

"But Doctor, if you do that he'll never be able to do anything for himself."

"Now, now, Mrs. Williamson," consoled the physician, "he'll be able to do everything he ever did . . .except play the piano. And after all, it's not so terribly important that he play the piano when you consider . . . "

At this moment Arthur himself revived feebly—enough to mutter, "I heard. I heard what he said. But I'll show him. I've played, I've played the piano ever since I was a kid; and I'm not going to give up *now*."

And Arthur Williamson did not give up. Arthur Williamson kept trying. When the bandages were removed he painfully searched the familiar keys with his stumps. Days of practice, hours of transposing into new keys . . . until with his unbroken spirit he re-mastered the instrument he loved.

Today, happily married, the father of two charming daughters, a successful piano salesman and a skillful pianist, Arthur Williamson has proved that it can be done.

How do you tackle your work each day?
    Are you scared of the job you find?
Do you grapple the task that comes your way
    With a confident, easy mind?
Do you stand right up to the work ahead

Or fearfully pause to view it?
Do you start to toil with a sense of dread
  Or feel that you're going to do it?

You can do as much as you think you can,
  But you'll never accomplish more;
If you're afraid of yourself, young man,
  There's little for you in store.
For failure comes from the inside first,
  It's there if we only knew it,
And you can win, though you face the worst,
  If you feel that you're going to do it.

Success! It's found in the soul of you,
  And not in the realm of luck!
The world will furnish the work to do,
  But you must provide the pluck.
You can do whatever you think you can,
  It's all in the way you view it.
It's all in the start that you make, young man:
  You must feel that you're going to do it.

How do you tackle your work each day?
  With confidence clear, or dread?
What to yourself do you stop and say
  When a new task lies ahead?
What is the thought that is in your mind?
  Is fear ever running through it?
If so, just tackle the next you find
  By thinking you're going to do it.
                    —*How Do You Tackle Your Work?*

[19]

THE COMMON TOUCH

I would not be too wise—so very wise
   That I must sneer at simple songs and creeds,
And let the glare of wisdom blind my eyes
   To humble people and their humble needs.

I would not care to climb so high that I
   Could never hear the children at their play,
Could only see the people passing by,
   Yet never hear the cheering words they say.

I would not know too much—too much to smile
   At trivial errors of the heart and hand,
Nor be too proud to play the friend the while,
   And cease to help and know and understand.

I would not care to sit upon a throne,
   Or build my house upon a mountain-top.
Where I must dwell in glory all alone
   And never friend come in or poor man stop.

God grant that I may live upon this earth
   And face the tasks which every morning brings,
And never lose the glory and the worth
   Of humble service and the simple things.

WOMAN OF IRON

STEEL for sale! Such a cry, coming from the lips of a trim, well-poised woman, is a strange sound indeed; yet it is no stranger than any chapter in the life of Mrs. Jean O'Haver Shassere, one of America's most extraordinary and most successful women. Mrs. Shassere, homemaker and mother, is of all things one of the world's foremost salesmen of reinforcing steel.

Thirty years ago, back in the first decade of the Twentieth Century, there was in Farmersburg, Indiana a beautiful young woman of twenty-two, the mother of two tiny children . . . a widow.

One day she had occasion to make a call on the telephone for a Tom Brown.

"Tom Brown? Which Tom Brown?" asked the operator. "There are five of them, you know."

"The one who works for the Hopkins," explained Mrs. Shassere, at the same time getting an idea. "Say," she said, "it wouldn't be such a bad idea if we had a telephone directory here in Farmersburg, would it?"

"It'd be a blessing," agreed the friendly operator. "But who'd pay for it?"

Young, active, aggressive Mrs. Shassere had a way of following up her ideas. She went to the head of the telephone company, only to be repulsed by the statement: "Of course we'd like to have a telephone directory, but our company can't afford to pay for it. And that's that."

She went next to the editor of the newspaper and told him of her idea of having the paper print the Farmersburg directory with local advertising in it to pay for the printing. "I'll guarantee the cost," she told him. "And stand the loss, if there is a loss."

"*If* there's a loss?" retorted the editor. "You're mighty optimistic, Mrs. Shassere."

But Mrs. Shassere went to the merchants and sold them on the idea that everyone who saw the directory would see their ads. And thus she accomplished the seemingly impossible. She gave Farmersburg its first telephone directory, engaging in business and at the same time successfully managing a home and feeding and clothing her children.

This, however, was only a start for this energetic, ambitious young woman. Soon other towns heard of her telephone directory and sought her out. She became advertising manager of a newspaper in a day when women solicitors were eyed askance. She traveled, worked hard, saved her money and put her children through school in Terre Haute.

They were in high school when one wintry day Mrs. Shassere was riding on a Terre Haute street car. In the blinding snow as she stood at the door, the motorman inquired, "Off here, lady?"

"No, next block, please," replied Mrs. Shassere.

"O.K. If we can make the corner," answered the motorman. "The snow's coming down so fast I no sooner pull down the window and wipe it off than it gets all blurred up again with the snow and ice."

"What you need," observed Mrs. Shassere," is a windshield wiper, like they have on automobiles."

"Sure they ought. Somebody'd make a lot of money if he invented one. But probably there's a bug in the idea somewhere, or somebody'd have it done. Probably it can't be done."

Mrs. Shassere tried her hand at inventing. When she had finished her windshield wiper she took it to the head of Rose Polytechnic Institute to find out if it was foolproof.

"Well, Mrs. Shassere," she was told, "as near as I can see, your invention is one hundred per cent. I only hope you have less trouble manufacturing it than we're having getting steel for our new school buildings."

"Trouble—getting steel?" answered Mrs. Shassere with a nose for business.

"Yes," explained the president of Rose Poly, "you see it comes from Indianapolis, and shipments . . . "

"From Indianapolis? But why don't you buy your steel here in Terre Haute?"

"Because there isn't a single company selling steel in the city."

Mrs. Shassere followed up that idea, too. Promptly she called the Gage Structural Steel Company in Chicago. Even before she had sold her windshield wiper to a car manufacturer in St. Louis, she had convinced Major Gage that she could land a big steel contract for him. "Don't be disappointed," Major Gage told her, "if you don't land it. You know, that's a pretty big hunk you've bitten off for yourself—selling steel. Between the two of us, that's a man's business."

"So they tell me, Major," agreed Mrs. Shassere, "but just wait till a *woman* gets into it."

The next thing anybody knew, Mrs. Shassere was after the steel contract for the new Merchandise Mart in Chicago—the biggest order for steel in the entire world. And she got it! Six thousand tons of reinforcing steel and two thousand tons of steel mesh. In addition, she actually designed the steel inserts on the building herself. The very next day after she sold the steel for the new Marshall Field building in Chicago, she sold the steel for the Board of Trade building. Previous to that, she sold the steel for the Passavant Hospital—each a monumental task in itself.

Yes, Jean O'Haver Shassere found that a woman could sell steel—even as a woman could sell country town telephone directories. In seventeen years she became one of America's biggest steel sellers.

In addition, her family has followed success with her. Today her daughter is Superintendent of the Belmont Hospital in Chicago, and her son is a successful newspaper man. And as a hobby, she has a leaning toward the creation of verse, of which the following is an example:

> To the man or woman striving
> To win out by just sheer pluck,

I say—don't take it on the chin
But learn instead to duck.

And as you come up—face the foe,
    Never falter but stand toe to toe,
For facing troubles makes them go,
    We reap the courage that we sow.

THE KINDLY NEIGHBOR

I have a kindly neighbor, one who stands
    Beside my gate and chats with me awhile,
    Gives me the glory of his radiant smile
And comes at times to help with willing hands.
No station high or rank this man commands,
    He, too, must trudge, as I, the long day's mile;
    And yet, devoid of pomp or gaudy style,
He has a worth exceeding stocks or lands.

To him I go when sorrow's at my door,
    On him I lean when burdens come my way,
Together oft we talk our trials o'er
    And there is warmth in each good-night we say.
A kindly neighbor! Wars and strife shall end
When man has made the man next door his friend.

THE CALL

I must get out to the woods again, to the whispering tree,
  and the birds a-wing,
Away from the haunts of pale-faced men, to the spaces
  wide where strength is king;
I must get out where the skies are blue and the air is
  clean and the rest is sweet,
Out where there's never a task to do or a goal to reach
  or a foe to meet.

I must get out on the trails once more that wind through
  shadowy haunts and cool,
Away from the presence of wall and door, and see myself
  in a crystal pool;
I must get out with the silent things, where neither
  laughter nor hate is heard,
Where malice never the humblest stings and no one is
  hurt by a spoken word.

Oh, I've heard the call of the tall white pine, and heard
  the call of the running brook;
I'm tired of the tasks which each day are mine, I'm weary
  of reading a printed book;
I want to get out of the din and strife, the clang and
  clamor of turning wheel,
And walk for a day where life is life, and the joys are
  true and the pictures real.

GOOBER MAN

How often we are prone to say, "But he had a break" or "Luck came his way." True enough, in some cases, but not so in the life of Dr. George Washington Carver, a name given high honor and esteem both in America and across the sea. Truly a noble man, George Washington Carver was born in the humblest circumstances—way back in the troublous days when the United States was torn into a North and a South.

Many have been the transformations America has undergone since those war-torn days, countless the advancements made possible by science; yet it remained for a negro child, born of slave parents—George Washington Carver by name—to give to all mankind the priceless gifts born of his scientific brain.

It was Dr. Carver who took peanuts, once a thing to be sold at circuses, and from them developed more than three hundred useful products. The lowly sweet potato has furnished Dr. Carver the basis for more than a hundred products. Millions upon millions of dollars in industry have resulted from his years of laboratory work. But not one penny has this famed and revered scientist taken from his labors. His is truly a great heart whose love for humanity carries him far beyond the reach of the dollar.

Humble indeed was George Washington Carver's birth. Born in a slave cabin, his birthright that of a child in bonds, his color black, Dr. Carver's achievements assume greater import from these facts. The odds were against him from the hour of his birth, and the next event in his life piled those odds even higher.

In the last year of the war between the states, came an invasion of slave raiders, and to the tiny, frail negro child was brought the taste of war's bitter cup. Snatched from his mother's arms by slave raiders, he was carried far from his home plantation. His master, George Carver, a kindly man who had always dealt tenderly with his slaves, began the task of recovering baby George and his mother and father. Being in straightened circumstances, however, Mr. George Carver had little to offer for their return. Nevertheless, he did locate baby George and for his return traded a horse together with a small sum of money. The mother and father he was never able to locate. They were never heard from again.

So the motherless little boy returned to his master's home to be raised there. Obtaining his education from a spelling book until he was ten years old, he secured employment on a neighboring farm and was able to attend rural school for one year. Then in his quest for knowledge, he turned his footsteps toward Fort Scott, Kansas, working as a domestic servant for nine years.

From there one day he decided to go to Minneapolis to continue his education. Even then he was interested in plants. He entered high school in Minneapolis, finished his course and started work as manager of a laundry. At night he would go to the library and study. Next he proceeded to Simpson College, at Indianola, Iowa, and three years later found him in Iowa State College at Ames, Iowa. Always working, always studying, he took first his Bachelor of Arts degree, then his Master's.

Presently he was placed in charge of the greenhouse at Ames, and then he was given charge of the bacteriological laboratory and the department of systematic botany. He was the first colored man to be put at the head of anything at Iowa State. He soon made his department at Iowa State outstanding, and as a result another great member of his race, the immortal Booker T. Washington, heard of his work and asked him to join the faculty at Tuskegee Institute.

"It may mean financial sacrifice," Booker T. Washington explained, in making the offer. "The prestige may not be so great."

"Mr. Washington," said Dr. Carver, "I'm honored. I'd be delighted to go to Tuskegee to continue my work. The financial end doesn't matter to me. I'm interested in the same thing you are—doing my best to further the interests of mankind, of our people; and, if possible, to add a little more to human knowledge."

And that's exactly what George Carver has devoted his life to—the interests of all mankind and the betterment of the negro race. Taking charge of the agriculture department at Tuskegee, he built it into national renown. In his laboratories, he spent long days and nights in delving into the by-products of those two typical edibles of the South, the lowly peanut and the familiar sweet potato.

Eventually in recognition of his contributions to science

he was made a Fellow of The Royal Society of Great Britain. Thus rose the child of slave parents to the foremost rank in the field of science and learning . . . to pre-eminence in his chosen field.

Later, advanced in years but still youthful in spirit, he was called on to address the members of the Ways and Means Committee of the House of Representatives on the use and possibilities of the peanut when a high tariff threatened to halt the import of the nut. "Substitute milk and butter," he told them in his conclusion, "are but two of the many by-products we hope to derive from this source."

His very progress in this field seems to have been a part of the evolution of things. Cotton was long the main crop of the South, but with the advent of the boll weevil, which destroyed practically the entire cotton crop, it became necessary to find something else to plant instead. Peanuts and sweet potatoes filled this need.

But increasing peanut production brought the requirement of also increasing peanut consumption. This led to searching for by-products of the peanut, some of the principal ones of which are flour, paints, dyes, plastics, peanut oils, peanut meats, various new confections. In 1896, the peanut industry of the South was so insignificant that it was not even listed in the industrial activities of the South. Today it is a $16,000,000 industry.

Furthermore, peanut oil has proved useful in the massage of atrophied muscles. "I have seen," Dr. Carver relates, "grown men carried into Tuskegee Institute, who through massage and the use of peanut oil, have regained their legs and have walked out sturdy and strong. I have also had others come to me with either both or one leg in a brace, and still others walking with crutches or canes, who have thrown them away after a number of treatments. Now, approximately ninety per cent of my work is concerned with infantile paralysis."

From the sweet potato, Dr. Carver has developed such products as mock coconut, starch, molasses, dyes and other products. As a side-line hobby, Dr. Carver paints in oils, using paints made from the two edibles he has done so much work with, the goober and the yam.

The thing dearest to his heart, however, is the foundation which has been established for the erection of the Carver Creative Research Laboratory. "By the founding of such an institution," he explains, "we can house a museum that may prove of great value to those who follow after me. I am simply a trail blazer, blazing a tiny trail that I hope may be widened by those who follow."

A thing of tubes and wires, and lo!
The miracle of radio!
The simple dial turning round
Searches the atmosphere for sound
And captures from the silent air
Song, music, eloquence and prayer.

How strange this mystery of things
Which to mankind such pleasure brings

[31]

And day and night with cheer illumes
The dreariest and loneliest rooms!
I never turn the dials round
But what I feel a thrill profound.

Fed by the magic microphones
The air takes up its freight of tones
And carries safely every word
Till nation wide the voice is heard.
A singer in New York appears
And distant California hears.

Oh, happier world, where all may know
The miracle of radio!
These things of tubes and wires now grace
The mansion and the cottage place
And rich and poor alike may share
The golden harvest of the air.

—*Radio*

HOT TOMATOES

"Too old to learn new tricks, too young to undertake life's serious problems." Most of us find it easy to excuse ourselves for our failures, but what about those who, in the face of handicap, went on with the task ahead of them with unfaltering courage?

Walter and Thornton Snead, twins from Evanston, Illinois, forced from college during the dark depression years and with no sign of employment, faced the future determined to succeed.

Raised by their father from boyhood on the premise that "one has to work in this world; everyone must put something into it before he can get anything out of it," the Snead twins were not overwhelmed when the depression struck. Throughout their childhood they had kept themselves occupied part of the time selling pop or Christmas trees. Through grade school and high school, they continued to turn their hands to job after job successfully. Then they left for Dartmouth College.

Returning home after their freshman year, in the summer of 1931, they found conditions greatly altered in their comfortable home.

"You mean, Dad," exclaimed Walter, "the depression has . . . "

"Made it impossible for me to help you next year at school," revealed Mr. Snead. "I'm sorry, but there's no way out that I can see. If you want to go back to Dart-

[33]

mouth next year, you'll have to make your own way!"

Undaunted, the boys found their inspiration at the dinner table. "Gee, Mom," gloated Walter, "this is sure good tomato juice."

"It sure is," seconded his brother Thornton. "I didn't know you made it yourself. I thought you always bought tomato juice in a can."

"You can buy it canned," agreed their mother, "if you have the money. But home made tastes better to your dad and me, anyway."

"H'm, that gives me an idea, Walter," spoke up Thornton. "There should be money in tomato juice, the good home-made kind."

"Why, that's our chance to go into business," applauded Walter.

"But we've got to make the best juice from selected tomatoes."

"The kind they grow from selected seeds. If we can just get the whole body of the tomatoes into the juice we'll have a richer product."

"And sell it direct to the home," appended Thornton.

"We'll get our friends to help us, too," added Walter.

The Snead twins never finished college. The Morning Glory Whole Tomato Beverage became such a thriving business that it called them back from the classrooms at Dartmouth. They called their product Morning Glory because as they say "no matter how you feel the 'morning after' a glass of Morning Glory will make you feel glorious."

[34]

And today in Evanston, Illinois a fine, modern building houses the business of the Snead brothers and their young partner, Leonard Burgweger, who joined the business in 1935 after leaving Yale. The business that began in their mother's sink is today one of America's foremost rising young enterprises, selling five different products.

In explanation of the rapid advance of their concern, Walter Snead says that it is due to "a number of reasons. For one thing, our four products have been developed to a point of perfection, and we have never lost sight of fundamentals, such as taking two of the oldest fruits and vegetables known, the prune and the tomato, and with the modern methods of packing, made them delicious and healthful to drink. By those means we have won the faith of buyers of some of the country's largest institutions, the faith of our two splendid banks and of the many firms that supply us with our materials."

The company packs only in glass bottles, either in their own or the dairies', and can turn out 6,000 pint bottles a day. In addition to Morning Glory, their first product, they have Plum Mellow Prune Juice and two other products—Plumps, which are "ready-to-eat-prunes," not unlike fresh fruit, and Colonel Bob's Virginia Sauce.

Consumption of tomato juice has risen from 185,000 cases of all sizes in 1929 to over twelve and a half million cases in 1936, and the Snead twins believe that prune juice today is in relatively the same position as tomato juice was ten years ago.

[35]

"I'm not a philosopher, bearded and gray,"
 Said he unto me.
"I'm simple of speech and I'm plain in my way,
 Which is easy to see.
I don't know the whys and the wherefores and whences,
That life really is and just how it commences,
But I do know the living encounter expenses.

"With high-sounding language I cannot compete,
 But some things I've learned.
I know that the money for house rent and meat
 Must always be earned.
And whether the man be day-toiler or scholar,
If his need be for coal or a tie for his collar
He must either have credit, or dig up the dollar.

"I know that I live and shall live till I die,
 And I don't have to read
Deep volumes to tell me as time hurries by
 There is much I shall need.
My problem is this: in foul weather or sunny,
My children will frequently want bread and honey
And the grocer who sells them will ask for the money.

"So having to live on the earth day by day,
 Along with the rest,
The problem's not which is the easiest way,
 But which is the best.

[36]

My philosophy's this: to look after my fences,
To think of the future before it commences
And to work for an income to meet life's expenses."
—His Philosophy

ACCOMPLISHED CARE

All things grow lovely in a little while,
  The brush of memory paints a canvas fair;
The dead face through the ages wears a smile,
  And glorious becomes accomplished care.

There's nothing ugly that can live for long,
  There's nothing constant in the realm of pain;
Right always comes to take the place of wrong,
  Who suffers much shall find the greater gain.

Life has a kindly way, despite its tears
  And all the burdens which its children bear;
It crowns with beauty all the troubled years
  And soothes the hurts and makes their memory fair.

Be brave when days are bitter with despair,
  Be true when you are made to suffer wrong;
Life's greatest joy is an accomplished care,
  There's nothing ugly that can live for long.

LIFE

Life is a jest;
    Take the delight of it.
Laughter is best;
    Sing through the night of it.
Swiftly the tear
    And the hurt and the ache of it
Find us down here;
    Life must be what we make of it.

Life is a song;
    Let us dance to the thrill of it.
Grief's hours are long,
    And cold is the chill of it.
Joy is man's need;
    Let us smile for the sake of it.
This be our creed:
    Life must be what we make of it.

Life is a soul;
    The virtue and vice of it.
Strife for a goal,
    And man's strength is the price of it.
Your life and mine,
    The bare bread and the cake of it,
End in this line:
    Life must be what we make of it.

BUSY FINGERS

"Knit one, purl two"—such is the familiar refrain of American women as they knit their way, day after day, in cars, on trains, even in motion picture theaters. Mrs. Violette Payne, proprietor of the Knitting Bowl in West-field, New Jersey knows that refrain, too. But it remained for Mrs. Payne to add to those words the courage and conviction that knitting needles and yarn could become a flourishing home business.

Mrs. Payne, social worker and woman's club enthusiast, blazed the way for the Knitting Bowl when, faced by drastically reduced circumstances, she found her scale of living slipping and determined to do something about it.

A few years ago Mrs. Payne, as program chairman of the Westfield Woman's Club, was attending a convention at Atlantic City. In company with a group of other delegates, she was walking down the board walk when one of the women proposed, "Let's rest. I'm tired."

"Oh, no. Not yet," answered one of the others. "Let's walk some more."

"Oh, look at that perfectly divine dress in that shop window," enthusiastically remarked a third lady.

"Which one? Oh, yes . . . I see it. The knit, there."

"I wish I could knit. You can make the loveliest things."

"Let's go in there," suggested Mrs. Payne. "I'd like to see some more of their things."

"No, let's not, Violette," held back one of the women. can't afford . . . "

"What's the use of going in, Mrs. Payne?" said another. "If you can't knit, seeing all those lovely things will only make you feel bad."

"You all go on and walk ahead if you want to," said Mrs. Payne. "I'm going in."

"But what . . . I mean what for, Violette?"

"For two reasons," Mrs. Payne explained. "I'd like to inquire about the cost. I mean costs for making some things for my two daughters. And besides, don't you think it would be a grand idea to start a knitting club for the women in the Westfield Club?"

"That's what I call inviting trouble," was the response of one of her friends.

"I'll say," said another. "You'll get them started knitting, and then they'll all quit."

"One by one. You know how women are."

"And then they'll blame you for getting them to spend money for the yarn."

But Violette Payne was not to be dissuaded by the gloomy thoughts of her friends. She believed that other women, like herself, hard hit by the depression, would welcome the opportunity to learn to knit clothes for themselves and their families.

Mrs. Payne was not only the instigator of the new knitting club, but she became the instructor as well. She helped her friends learn how to do the difficult shoulders of the garments. Furthermore, she managed to borrow $250

[40]

on her husband's insurance and, although informed that at least a thousand dollars in capital would be needed to finance a knit-shop, she convinced the company executive to make the try.

In addition, she proved to her friends that it was fun to knit—and profitable, too. And so today in Westfield, New Jersey stands the Knitting Bowl. There, every hour of the day, you may find Mrs. Payne and her group of assistants, planning, designing, instructing. For a while she did all of the designing herself, but now all of her ten assistants do designing.

Mrs. Payne accounts for the growth of the Knitting Bowl by saying that she believes that "every customer is our most valuable asset. It is not enough to sell her yarn; we think first of all about design, individual design. Too often a woman enthuses over knitting only to find her knitting such, when finished, that it does not become her."

The knitting for the Bowl is done by professional knitters in their homes—fifteen to twenty of them, all of whom had never knitted before. While a success in business, Mrs. Payne has found no need to neglect her family, her husband and two fine daughters.

"If you have a burning desire to succeed," she advises from her experiences, "know the business you are planning to enter; work hard and long and, above all, keep faith with your customers. They are the asset of any business."

Forty-five years of age, Mrs. Violette Payne has literally knitted her way to fame, and the modern, up-to-date Knitting Bowl, Westfield's favorite rendezvous, is the

result of ten busy fingers, one active brain and an un-
limited amount of courage and belief that it could be done.

One broken dream is not the end of dreaming,
　　One shattered hope is not the end of all,
Beyond the storm and tempest stars are gleaming,
　　Still build your castles, though your castles fall.

Though many dreams come tumbling in disaster,
　　And pain and heartache meet us down the years,
Still keep your faith, your dreams and hopes to master
　　And seek to find the lesson of your tears.

Not all is as it should be! See how littered
　　With sorry wreckage is life's restless stream.
Some dreams are vain, but be you not embittered
　　And never cry that you have ceased to dream!
　　　　　　　　　　　　　　　　—Dreams

BABY CHICKS

"HE Glorified the American Chicken" might well be the title of the life-story of Milton H. Arndt, Battery Brood Specialist of Trenton, New Jersey. It was Mr. Arndt who raised the breeding of chickens from a haphazard, unscientific practice to the precise, hygienic venture it is today.

Son of a midwestern farmer, Mr. Arndt worked his way through high school and college selling eggs. Followed a series of jobs, then a job in a Philadelphia grocery store, which he lost because of his attention to a brood of chicks he was raising in the back yard.

On the side, while selling insurance, he still tried raising chickens—chickens which died so fast that as Mr. Arndt recalls, "I had to devote most of my time to selling insurance, so I could afford to pay the losses on my chickens."

Two old ladies raising canaries in Trenton, each bird in its own cage, gave Milton Arndt the idea that eventually led him to success. "If you'll only let me show you the cages I've built," he enthusiastically pleaded with the head of a big company raising chickens. "I've proved that it can be done, sir. My chickens are healthier. They're more free from disease. The mortality rate isn't so high. If you'll only give me a chance to prove my ideas to your customers, why, it'll revolutionize the whole chicken business."

After the tryout, Arndt was let out. "But hasn't my work proved satisfactory?" he insisted. "Haven't you seen how the chickens thrived in their individual cages?"

"That isn't the point," he was told. "The point is that we're in the business of selling baby chicks. What happens to them after they're sold isn't our business. And we're losing trade because all our customers are laughing at your crazy ideas."

So he went home and said to his wife, "I want you to look the whole thing square in the face, honey. We've got exactly $470. And if we follow my plans and open a factory in Trenton to make chicken cages—and all the rest of my ideas—we, well, we may go broke."

"Well, we've been broke before, dear," courageously replied Mrs. Arndt. "I'm ready to take the chance if you are."

"But you *do* realize that everybody says it can't be done, that people have always let their chickens run loose and get sick and die. And that we'll have to pioneer the way."

"Yes, I know," she said. "But *somebody* always has to pioneer."

Thus a man and a woman who believed that it could be done went to Trenton, New Jersey and opened a tiny place of business. And because the idea was good, because they believed they could do it, the Milton H. Arndt plan for raising chickens in individual cages, in ventilated and even-temperature chicken houses, thrived and prospered.

The Arndt "battery" plant is a series of cages, each one built for a definite size of bird and all housed in an air-conditioned and heated plant. The chickens are put into a cage when they are one day old and then they graduate from machine to machine until they reach maturity at about five months of age. Then each one is put into its own individual cage where it spends the balance of its life.

The system has been operating commercially since 1929, following three years of experimentation before that. With this system a thousand birds in a building thirty by sixty will supply a person a decent living.

In his own two plants, one of which covers a quarter of an acre, accommodating 16,000 birds, and another ninety acres on which are 19,000, he has radios in his chicken houses. "We find that it increases production by about ten per cent," he says. "We have the chickens get up in the morning with their setting-up exercises, then they have their domestic science lectures, luncheon music, political speeches in the afternoon, although the chickens don't like them, and in the evening we put them to bed with their bedtime story."

Since these chickens do not run out in the sunlight, they are fed a definite amount of cod liver oil each day to supply the sunlight factor of Vitamin "D."

Today one of Trenton's leading industries is the M. H. Arndt Manufacturing Company. Throughout America, products of the Arndt Company are used by leading chicken farms. And, as Milton Arndt is wont to say, if the

chickens could talk to you from their New Era cages,
they would say: "See, it can be done!"

If to grumbling you're inclined
   Every time a plan goes wrong,
Grumble on and ease your mind,
   But keep plodding right along.
Grit your teeth and wear a frown,
   But keep walking straight ahead.
There's no sense in lying down
   Till it's time to go to bed.

If ill luck has come your way,
   Keep on fighting as you sigh;
While with wailing loss you stay
   Life's parade goes marching by.
Never mind what's come and gone,
   Waste no time on chances fled;
Forward march and carry on.
   Do your lying down in bed!

When misfortune deals a blow,
   Be your body bruised and black,
There is just one way to go;
   There can be no turning back.

[46]

While you've strength to walk the town
  Stand up straight and look ahead.
There's no sense in lying down
  Till it's time to go to bed.
                    —*On Lying Down*

SUCCESS

This I would claim for my success—not fame nor gold,
  Nor the throng's changing cheers from day to day,
  Not always ease and fortune's glad display,
Though all of these are pleasant joys to hold;
But I would like to have my story told
  By smiling friends with whom I've shared the way,
Who, thinking of me, nod their heads and say:
"His heart was warm when other hearts were cold.

"None turned to him for aid and found it not,
  His eyes were never blind to man's distress.
Youth and old age he lived, nor once forgot
  The anguish and the ache of loneliness;
His name was free from stain or shameful blot
And in his friendship men found happiness."

LIVING

The miser thinks he's living when he's hoarding up his
  gold;
The soldier calls it living when he's doing something bold;
The sailor thinks it living to be tossed upon the sea,
And upon this very subject no two men of us agree.
But I hold to the opinion, as I walk my way along,
That living's made of laughter and good-fellowship and
  song.

I wouldn't call it living to be always seeking gold,
To bank all the present gladness for the days when I'll
  be old.
I wouldn't call it living to spend all my strength for fame,
And forego the many pleasures which today are mine to
  claim.
I wouldn't for the splendor of the world set out to roam,
And forsake my laughing children and the peace I know
  at home.

Oh, the thing that I call living isn't gold or fame at all!
It's fellowship and sunshine, and it's roses by the wall.
It's evenings glad with music and a hearth-fire that's
  ablaze,
And the joys which come to mortals in a thousand dif-
  ferent ways.
It is laughter and contentment and the struggle for a goal;
It is everything that's needful in the shaping of a soul.

ANIMATED SIGNS

SIGNS for sale! Signs that move, that walk, skip, run and jump—signs that stop you! Such is the story of Douglas Leigh, and Douglas Leigh is just a young man, at twenty-seven the toast of skeptical New York. Mr. Leigh is the typical small-town boy who made good in the big city, in a big, big way. This boy from Anniston, Alabama actually "lit up" Broadway's Great White Way.

He has thrown huge animated signs against the sides of buildings; he has done the spectacular in America's most spectacular city, and in doing it he has again proved to every American, young or old, that "It Can Be Done!"

As a boy back in Anniston, Alabama Douglas Leigh early displayed a knack for selling things such as magazines and knick-knacks. Then at the University of Florida he showed the same talent. He patented an alligator belt and sold it to all the men on the campus. He sold ads for the year book and Masqueraders' programs. He devised a tiny alligator with its mouth open for football souvenirs, proving time and again that he was a young fellow who kept his eyes open. He "worked his way through college" and was an outstanding financial success. But the lights that were to spell his name had only begun to glow.

Then his family moved to Birmingham, Alabama, but after selling signs awhile for Mr. Holt, Leigh quit his job and went over to Atlanta. "I can't understand," said the man to whom he applied for a job, "why, when you're doing so well with Holt over in Birmingham, you want to join us here in Atlanta, at less money."

"You see," explained Leigh, "there are two reasons. First, you people are in outdoor advertising, and I want to get into that branch. And second, what I'm looking for is opportunity. Just give me that and if I don't make more money, it'll just be my own fault."

However, later on when Leigh asked for a raise on the score of a good sales record, he was turned down. With that he announced, "I'm quitting! I'm going to New York!"

"Don't do that, son," he was advised. "You know, you're a pretty big frog in our pond down here in Atlanta; but in New York . . ."

So Douglas Leigh headed for America's largest metropolis, to conquer New York with a heart full of courage and ambition and a pocketbook containing eight dollars and fifty-two cents. But courage and ambition were apparently more important than financial resources, and the will-to-do was apparently weightier than a slim bankroll, for the young southerner soon was working for a great outdoor sign company, working in Brooklyn and spending his nights on gay Broadway.

While walking with a girl friend along the Great White Way, he was chided: "Come on, Doug; anybody'd take you for a hick from the sticks the way you keep on staring at those signs."

[50]

"I *am* a hick from the sticks," Doug conceded. "Just a small-town boy out to see the big city. Hey, look at that sign across the street. Watch it flash on and off!"

The girl: (mockingly) " 'Look at that sign!' 'Look at that one!' Listen, Doug, you're a nice guy and I like you, but I'm sick of looking at signs."

"I'm not," he retorted. "Some day I'm gonna *build* a big sign, a spectacular . . . "

"Some day you're going to *marry* a big sign, and it'd serve you right, too. I never saw such a guy, with such nutty ideas. Next thing I hear you'll be going in business for yourself."

Doug was not very long in following out that idea. The depression came, and he was asked to take a cut, which he refused to do. He quit and in a small way started in the sign business for himself. It was no smooth, easy road. On the contrary, it was fight, fight every inch of the way, driving, bargaining, believing that it could be done. Soon another sign joined his first effort, and then another and another; and young Douglas Leigh had arrived in the Big City in a "big way."

But he wasn't through yet. The young dynamo was just beginning to gain power. As the great sign men of New York discussed a European visitor, Douglas Leigh listened.

"His name's Kurt Rosenberg," said one. "He's an Austrian. Tried out his animated sign idea in Stockholm, Sweden and . . . "

"I know," replied another of the advertising men. "He's

here now to sell it to America. But it won't work! It can't be done!"

"That's right. The time's not ripe. The . . . "

"Rosenberg, did you say?" spoke up Leigh.

"That's right, Leigh. Why?"

"Oh, nothing. Only I thought I'd go have a talk with him. You see, in spite of what you all say, gentlemen, I think it can be done!"

Famous for its traffic jams, New York was not long in obtaining bigger and better traffic jams, thanks to Douglas Leigh.

"Keep movin', keep movin' there! Don't block the traffic," the cops would bellow to pedestrians pausing in front of Leigh's new animated signs to watch the fun.

"Oh, isn't that a marvelous sign?" a woman would comment. "Did you ever see more lights in your life?"

"Oh, Mom! Mom!" gurgled her child. "Look! It's like a cartoon comedy! Lookit that funny elephant! And see the ducks coming out!"

Others commented, "Say, that sign *is* something. What won't they think up next?"

"You mean what won't Douglas Leigh think up next!"

"Douglas Leigh? Who's he?"

"The young fellow that thought up this sign! I was readin' in Winchell's column about him! Winchell says he wants to put up a sign on the Empire State Building! Make it look like a big cigarette! And he probably will, too."

Thus Douglas Leigh took the town with the Leigh-Epok

signs showing animated cartoons in lights, much like a movie, entertaining also like radio by using occasional commercial anouncements in light. As Mr. Leigh explains, "We have a duck chasing a bee, a horse that goes berserk now and then, an ostrich whose head and long neck become stuck in the sand, three cats in a fast and furious baseball game and the same cats in a football game. Walter Winchell calls it 'the best free show on Broadway.'"

On a movie screen three times the size of those in a picture house there will be as many as 4,000 light bulbs going on and off to form the different images. The apparatus uses a thousand electric eyes and looks not unlike a movie projector with a celluloid film. While most of the other signs on Broadway repeat themselves every thirty seconds with the same message day after day for three years, Leigh's new signs can show five minutes to an hour, with everything different, before it ever repeats itself. And then when it does become tiring, they merely create a new animated film, and it's a new show.

"We find," he says, "that the most successful bright light advertisements are those that do not take themselves too seriously. For instance, the cat playing with the ball of yarn, the chariot race, a winking penguin, etc. That is our real reason for using comics instead of serious subjects."

The Leigh-Epok system is capable of turning on and off as many as 104,000,000 electric impulses per hour. As a matter of fact, the Epok uses more electric eyes or photocells than any other modern invention, including sound systems or television, and each sign requires between 100,000 and 200,000 feet of wire.

One of Leigh's signs had a steaming cup of coffee. "And the first night we turned it on," he relates, "the steam turned to water and gave thousands of passersby a good soaking. As people passed that one spot, up went the umbrellas and on went the raincoats, while others stood by getting a great laugh."

"Here," says Mr. Leigh in explanation of the chance he took on the Epok system, "was an opportunity for the first time to give complete flexibility to an electric sign. We could do practically anything that the animated cartoons could do. We also can use movie trailers. In other words, I felt that America was craving today, as it had in years past, for entertainment and more entertainment, and we for the first time brought to electric signs complete entertainment coupled with brilliant electrical advertising. I felt that as long as there was a Broadway and a Times Square, there would always be electric signs."

Yes, New York has accepted Douglas Leigh and his animated signs. Today, twenty-seven years old, Mr. Leigh is President of Douglas Leigh, Incorporated—a busy company in a booming industry. And Douglas Leigh, President, repeats his favorite quotation when he turns his eyes toward the future. The late Arthur Brisbane said it, and it epitomizes this young man from the south and his attitude toward life: "What a man can imagine, a man can do!"

They say that luck follows a winner.
  That statement, I'm certain, is true.
The chap who wants fish for a dinner
  Must go where there's fishing to do.
He must be where the big ones can find him
  On the stream with the bait on his hook.
Who'd have luck must put wishing behind him
  And early be out on the brook.

It is vain to sit waiting and wishing
  For luck till the season is o'er.
Luck may find you some day when you're fishing
  But never 'twill come to the shore.
It is useless to grumble and pout there
  And wail that the signs are all wrong.
The lucky chap always is out there
  In case luck may happen along.

You'll be told that the winner is lucky!
  Believe me, the statement is true.
But also he's patient and plucky.
  His part he is willing to do.
He doesn't stay sulking and shirking
  Just waiting for luck to come by,
For the goal that he wants he keeps working.
  The first rule of luck is to try.
                    —*Why Winners Are Lucky*

[55]

THE ONE IN TEN

Nine passed him by with a hasty look,
   Each bent on his eager way;
One glance at him was the most they took,
   "Somebody stuck," said they;
But it never occurred to the nine to heed
A stranger's plight and a stranger's need.

The tenth man looked at the stranded car,
   And he promptly stopped his own.
"Let's see if I know what your troubles are,"
   Said he in a cheerful tone;
"Just stuck in the mire. Here's a cable stout,
Hitch onto my bus and I'll pull you out."

"A thousand thanks," said the stranger then,
   "For the debt that I owe you;
I've counted them all and you're one in ten
   Such a kindly deed to do."
And the tenth man smiled and he answered then,
"Make sure that you'll be the one in ten."

Are you one of the nine who pass men by
   In this hasty life we live?
Do you refuse with a downcast eye
   The help which you could give?
Or are you the one in ten whose creed
Is always to stop for the man in need?

RATTLESNAKE MEAT

GEORGE K. END's life story is a strange one—a life filled with excitement and over-brimming with the unusual. His achievement of popularizing rattlesnake meat as a delicacy of the dinner table is but another proof of what can be achieved through persistence and the will to win. He founded one of the strangest industries in the world, the Floridian Products Corporation, canners of rattlesnake meat.

Little did the residents of Sheboygan, Wisconsin think that their fellow townsman, George End, would set the lines of his life along the unusual until 1915 when word came that he was in far-off Serbia. The newspaper item said: "George K. End of Sheboygan, Wisconsin has joined the Columbia University Relief Expedition to Serbia, which was organized by Dr. Michael Pupin. Mr. End and his associates sail at once for Serbia to bring relief to residents of that war-torn Balkan country."

After the relief expedition disbanded and were on their way back to the States, George End found himself in Naples, Italy where he was suddenly and mistakenly arrested as a spy. Saved from the firing squad by the intervention of the American Consul, the adventurous youth joined the American field service with the French army, serving on the Aisne, Marne and Verdun fronts as an ambulance driver. George Kenneth End at the age of twenty-one had seen some tough moments.

There followed a period of service with the American ambulance branch in Serbia until the United States entered the war. With the declaration of America's entrance into the world's strife, George End was commissioned an officer and served in the American Expeditionary Forces until July, 1919.

At the age of twenty-five, he found himself in France, married, the father of a year-old son and engaged in the export business. Suddenly he decided to return to America where he worked for a while selling oil. He moved from job to job, never quite finding himself, until finally in October, 1927 he decided to turn his hand to farming.

"And you really think you can make a success of a truck farm?" asked a man at Arcadia, Florida. "You know, you're gonna have to fight a lot of things, including snakes—rattlesnakes."

"Well, I never did like snakes," replied George, "not since I was a kid. If you'll believe in me to the extent of grub-staking me, however, I know I can make a go of the farm and really have something for my wife and the two kids."

End promptly produced five acres of Patty Pan squash, only to find that there was no market for them, and the only thing he could do was to feed them to hogs. "I don't know what's wrong with me, Jenny," George complained to his wife at this low moment of his career. "It just seems that every time I do something it doesn't turn out right. We've got some fine hogs, but nobody wants to buy them."

"Don't blame yourself, George," replied Jenny. "You did what you thought was right, and that's all that matters."

"But I just can't let it rest at that. I guess I'll just have to take the rest of our grub stake money and buy a canning outfit to can the pork."

George End *did* buy the canning outfit, but again the Fates moved against him. A series of crop calamities finally exhausted the grub stake, and his ten acres of land at Arcadia, Florida became filled with weeds and rattlesnakes.

One day out in the patch he caught a whopper of a rattlesnake. "You know," George observed, "I've been studying these rattlers ever since I've been down here in Florida, and you know what I've found out?—they're among the cleanest creatures in the world. You know, some day I've got half a hunch to try *eating* one!"

For some time, George End continued his study of the fascinating rattler. Day after day, he studied his habits, amazed at the cleanliness of the flesh. Then one day in the spring of 1931 he and his two sons were in the kitchen of their farm house.

"Gosh, Daddy," spoke up one of the boys, "won't mother be awful mad?"

"She'll be fit to be tied," went on the second son, "usin' her pots and pans!"

"Well," put in George End, "don't you boys worry. This is my idea. I'll handle your mother. Let's see how our steaks are getting along."

"Gosh, look at 'em," continued one of his sons. "Rattlesnake steaks! You know, Dad, they look good enough to eat."

"Well," laughed George, "there's only one way to find out—that's to eat 'em. Come on, boys—remember the first American settlers found snake meat delicious. And, after all, aren't we pioneers, too?"

In telling of the experience later, George End said, "I not only ate it, but found it the best eating I've ever tasted. You know what?—I'll bet a fellow could make some nice money selling canned rattlesnake meat to a lot of folks, if he only had the money to get started."

Ever alert to find possibilities to expand his new business, George soon made plans to attend the Florida American Legion Convention. He took along some of his canned rattlesnake meat and gave a dinner at the Hillsborough Hotel. He found among the Legionnaires men game enough to follow his "lead" in eating rattlesnake meat.

Those Florida members of the American Legion didn't miss that feast. And thus was accomplished the first public acceptance of rattlesnake meat. They found it tasty, tender, different. Soon all America was to hear of this new food.

In the course of a year now Mr. End handles about two thousand rattlers, all genuine diamond-backs, averaging from three and a half to six feet in length and from five to twenty pounds in weight. He has hunters all over south Florida catching them and shipping them to him

alive. They are kept in a pen until the number is sufficient
to warrant canning them, which as a rule is within a week
or ten days because rattlers will not eat in captivity.

Rattlesnake meat now is served in almost all of the
fine restaurants and eating places and sold in the finest
stores throughout the country. The skins are converted
into leather which is made up into a variety of articles,
everything from ladies' sport jackets to purses, belts and
shoes. The backbones become souvenirs; the skulls are
dissected and sold as museum pieces. The fat is rendered
into oil for medicinal uses. The snake is milked of its
venom, and the venom is used in the preparation of anti-
venom and other scientific research. The "musk" has possibilities for use as a base for perfume.

Thus George K. End founded an enterprise which was
to bring him fame and fortune. All his life he had done
the impossible, so it did not look so tough to him when,
with $100 borrowed capital and a trusting printer, he
founded the Floridian Products Corporation at Tampa.
Today, rattlesnake meat is sought after by food con-
noiseurs everywhere. Today at Tampa, Mr. End has one
of the most interesting reptilian collections in the world.

I sing of the old-fashioned carver who gracefully wielded
    his blade,
Who sat in his place with a grin on his face and was
    deaf to the comment we made;
He had learned every joint of a chicken, a turkey, a par-
    tridge or goose,

And he sat there or stood as a gentleman should as he
cleverly whittled them loose.
Oh, there was an artist worth watching, a master per-
former was he;
But the age has grown smart, and that glorious art is a
joy that no longer we see.

My grandfather taught to my father the knack of dis-
secting a hen,
He made him recite where was dark meat and light again
and again and again.
He trained him to sharpen his knife on the steel, and to
flourish his blade in the air,
He shouted: "Alack! You do nothing but hack, when
you ought to be slicing with care."
'Twas a gentleman's boast as he sat at a roast that he
skillfully handled his knife;
And until a boy knew where the second joint grew he
wasn't thought ready for life.

Now they whittle the meat in the kitchen, and bring it
piled up on a plate;
Be it roast beef or ham, or a turkey or lamb, it is passed
in the ready-carved state.
And nobody jests with the carver, and nobody praises his
art;
There are grown men today who unblushingly say they
can't get a drum stick apart,

But something has gone from the dinner, however expensive its cost,
That we viewed with delight in the age taken flight, ere
the fine art of carving was lost.

—The Carver

A WARM HOUSE AND A RUDDY FIRE

A warm house and a ruddy fire,
To what more can man aspire?
Eyes that shine with love aglow,
Is there more for man to know?

Whether home be rich or poor,
If contentment mark the door
He who finds it good to live
Has the best that life can give.

This the end of mortal strife!
Peace at night to sweeten life,
Rest when mind and body tire,
At contentment's ruddy fire.

Rooms where merry songs are sung,
Happy old and glorious young;
These, if perfect peace be known,
Both the rich and poor must own.

A warm house and a ruddy fire,
These the goals of all desire,
These the dream of every man
Since God spoke and life began.

[63]

CLINCHING THE BOLT

It needed just an extra turn to make the bolt secure,
A few more minutes on the job and then the work was
    sure;
But he begrudged the extra turn, and when the task was
    through,
The man was back for more repairs in just a day or two.

Two men there are in every place, and one is only fair,
The other gives the extra turn to every bolt that's there;
One man is slip-shod in his work and eager to be quit,
The other never leaves a task until he's sure of it.

The difference 'twixt good and bad is not so very much,
A few more minutes at the task, an extra turn or touch,
A final test that all is right—and yet the men are few
Who seem to think it worth their while these extra things
    to do.

The poor man knows as well as does the good man how
    to work,
But one takes pride in every task, the other likes to shirk;
With just as little as he can, one seeks his pay to earn,
The good man always gives the bolt that clinching, extra
    turn.

SHOW WINDOWS

Sнips of jade, laden with jewels; ships that sail across a mirror sea toward a harbor made of lustrous pearls. No, such is not the stuff that dreams are made of; this is but a description of a jewelry store window, trimmed and decorated by Mrs. Polly Pettit, one of America's foremost window display designers.

The story of Polly Pettit is replete with the determination of an intelligent woman out to achieve the goal she had set for herself. Polly Pettit was not only a pioneer in the art of modern merchandising, she was a woman in a field hitherto strictly confined to men. Today she is a recognized authority in that field and is the originator and director of the New York School of Display, her last and greatest accomplishment.

Even at the tender age of seven, Polly Pettit showed signs of genius for decoration when one evening at her home in historic Dover, Delaware she surprised his mother's dinner guests with an ad lib decoration of the table with the bowl of goldfish in the middle and forks tied with red and green ribbons, to say nothing of the flowers on the salad!

But that year she lost her kind father whom she adored. Little Polly Pettit grew up, became a student of Dover High School, graduated from Northfield Seminary and married. Then came motherhood and eventually hard times. Polly Pettit was confronted with the problem of making money for the support of her child and the maintenance of her home.

First she went to a patent attorney with a new invention. "Here it is," she explained. "It's a paper tooth brush! I think it's a grand idea. You see, it can be sold in slot machines in rest rooms. And I've got another idea to go with it—each paper tooth brush will have a little sample tube of tooth paste right with it!"

But the patent attorney didn't think much of it, and so Polly just let it slide into the limbo of the lost. But she said, "I'm still not discouraged. I think that if I just keep on trying, I'll get an idea that will be good yet. You know, I believe that you have to fail, before you can really succeed."

Next she got a job with a big company in New York that was going to have food displays, and she was going to design them for the concern for three hundred dollars a month. That looked great, but unfortunately the company soon went bankrupt, and Mrs. Pettit again was out of a job.

Then she undertook to sell art work on a commission basis, but after six weeks of strenuous effort, an accounting showed that she owed the company exactly $44.65!

Such were the ingredients of Polly Pettit's career—disappointment, discouragement, failure; yet from these this courageous woman was to rise to a high rank in the field of display designing. Polly Pettit was a born crusader. From her early childhood she had endeavored in one way or another to accomplish the task she had outlined for herself. But the young wife and mother had not yet found the craft which was to make her famous. She had the determination, however, and the will to win, and these forces were to fashion her career.

One day, the day of her son's fifth birthday, she took the first step.

"What you doing, mommy?" asked the little boy at her side.

"Wait, John—you'll see," she told him. "Now, you see these gumdrops?"

"Ummm-humm. They're for my party. Can I have one?"

"Not just yet, dear. Now we put this little wire through here . . . like that . . . and we fasten one tooth pick here . . . and another here . . . and . . . "

"Mommy! Mommy!" excitedly cried the little boy. "It's a little gumdrop doll!"

"Yes," laughed Mrs. Pettit. "That's just what it is, John. Now we put a smile on his face, like that. And there he is!"

"Goody, goody! Let's make lots of 'em for all the kids! Golly, mommy, I'll bet every kid in the world will want one of these!"

Mrs. Pettit hoped so. She obtained a patent on the little gumdrop figures, registering each one, and sold them to a company on a royalty arrangement. In addition she was asked to join the company in the work of designing other candy novelties and arranging window displays.

That's how Polly Pettit got her foot on the first rung

of the ladder she was to climb. But Mrs. Pettit was not content to remain on the first rung. Rebuffed in an effort to get a job in the display department of a great store on New York's Fifth Avenue because she was a woman and the display business then was regarded as a man's field, she decided to open her own studio.

Soon she was in demand as one who could give a "woman's touch" to window display merchandising. A jewelry store window of her designing attracted crush crowds—it was a magic garden. Soon all New York was talking about Polly Pettit's unique and daring window displays. Her ideas had begun a new era in the method of showing merchandise behind glass. And Mrs. Pettit herself was growing along with her fame. She studied diligently and began to write articles on her work. Then she trained herself to become a public speaker that she might tell of her work.

When announcement was made of the selection of twenty-four "Women of Achievement" by the New York League of Business and Professional Women's Clubs, among those honored was Mrs. Polly Pettit.

Not satisfied with that much achievement, Mrs. Pettit next took the chance of starting a school of display because, as she said, "there are so many young men and women eager to learn new methods, new ideas, and because by opening a school I can help them."

Today at Rockefeller Center in New York, young men and women are studying modern merchandising methods in window and interior display at Polly Pettit's school.

Throughout America, graduates of her training course are occupying important positions in their chosen fields.

"Today I point with pride," says the first woman in the country to enter the window display business, "to a great many women who are doing grand jobs in window display work all over America. Sooner or later cities must learn to make their business streets beautiful because beauty sells. It's a modest ambition, but I would like to make the business streets beautiful from coast to coast, so we could boast about them and be proud of them. I want to encourage every young man and woman in this country with any decorative ability or a flair for working with their hands as well as their head, to think well about this very promising field of endeavor."

Back of every golden dream,
Every engine hissing steam,
Back of every hammer falling
And of every deed men dare;
Back of every tilt and fight
Is the coming home at night
To the loved ones who are waiting
In the victory to share.

When all is said and done
And the battle's lost or won,
It's the laughter of the children
And the mother's gentle smile,

It's the pride of those you know,
Good old friends who love you so,
That make the prize worth having
And the victory worth while.

'Tis not in success alone
That achievement's worth is known.
If we had no friends to cheer us
And no one at home to care;
If man's glory as a fighter
Did not make a few eyes brighter
He would cease to try for conquest
And would never do or dare.

Back of every man you'll find
Loving hearts who stay behind,
Watching, waiting, patient, loyal,
As he strives to meet the test,
And the thought which drives him daily
Is that they shall meet him gayly,
And shall glory in his triumph
On the day he does his best.

—Triumph

GANG BUSTER

Safeblowers get $50,000 in diamonds! Loft burglars escape with $35,000 in mink and silver fox furs!

Morning after morning the city of New York awakened to headlines like these, telling of the work of organized mobs plundering the lofts and vaults of gem merchants, of fur dealers, of optical firms where gold and platinum were their loot. And always they left the police baffled! How could the raids of these clever gangs be stopped? *Could* they be stopped? That was for Captain Richard Fennelly, head of the safe and loft squad of the New York City Police Department, to determine.

On a July morning in 1910 in the offices of an insurance firm on Broadway, a group of solicitors sat at their desks preparing their day's work when a stenographer said, "Mr. Fennelly, here's a letter for you . . . from the police department. I hope you're not in trouble?"

"I'm sure I'm not, Miss Barry," replied Fennelly with a laugh, "but we'll soon see." Fennelly opened the envelope, unfolded the letter and presently was shouting, "Hurray! Hurray! Fellows, I got my appointment! I got my appointment to the New York Police Department, as a patrolman!"

"You mean, you're going to be a copper?" asked one of his friends.

"That's right!"

"You're quitting the insurance business to be a flat-foot, to pick bananas off a fruit stand? What's the idea? You were doing all right here."

"Maybe I was," said Fennelly, "but I feel there's a real opportunity for a good man on the police force."

"Opportunity? Go on, you'll be just another cop among 10,000. Probably walk a beat the rest of your life."

"I don't think so. I think there's a place up the ladder for a young fellow who can think."

Four years later, Fennelly was called before the Commissioner of Police. "I've been reading over your record here," said the Commissioner. "On the police force four years. Made detective first year. Pretty good for a fellow with only a grade school education."

"That's all the schooling I could afford, sir," defended Fennelly.

"Hmm. Seems it hasn't held you back. Fennelly, there've been three delegations of business men in here today—the jewelers, furriers and opticians. Makes almost a dozen this week. They're driving me crazy with complaints about loft burglaries. Now you've had some luck lately rounding up some jewelry burglars . . . "

"It wasn't all luck, Commissioner," insisted Fennelly. "I've some pretty definite ideas on how to deal with those gangs."

"You have? That's good—because I'm giving you the job of breaking them up. It's a tough assignment, I know—even our veteran detectives haven't been able to stamp them out. You think you can do it?"

[72]

"I'll do my best, Commissioner," Fennelly promised. "I'd like some young detectives to help me, sir."

"All right, pick the men you want. But let's have some action."

Soon Fennelly's squad was called in to look over a jewelry robbery in Queens. The smart mob had beat the electric alarm by cutting a hole in the floor from upstairs. The only clue they picked up was a tip from a barber shop across the street that there was a dirty tan auto parked outside. Fennelly recalled that a similar car had been spotted in a burglary the previous week in White Plains.

So Fennelly's squad tackled the job of spotting a dirty tan sedan among the million cars in the city of New York. Then one day they did spot it, pulling up in front of a loft building. Out of the car stepped Blackie Stern and marched into the building just as if he belonged there.

From the porter of the building Fennelly learned that the gentleman was Mr. Steinberg, who was just looking over the building for the purpose of renting a loft for his jewelry business.

In conference with his men Fennelly decided: "I've got it! It's the building next door! Look! The optical house—Hall and Company. Opticians use a lot of gold and platinum. That's the stuff Blackie goes for. They're after the workshop on the second floor. That's where the vault is located."

Immediately Fennelly's men began to shadow Blackie to find out whom he was working with. From a bartender in a saloon, Fennelly learned that three yeggs in there with Blackie were Monk Hoffman, Mockie Moskowitz and Hank Bartelsky—all with records a mile long.

Soon the squad learned that the mob had bought four suitcases in a luggage shop; at a hardware store they bought an automatic machine hammer; at another store a brace and some drills; at a locksmith some keys had been made from a wax impression. A shop girl revealed that one of the yeggs had bought three yards of black oil cloth.

So Fennelly set his trap with fifteen men around the optical house. For eight hours they waited, only to learn in the end that they had been made chumps! While they were waiting to grab the mob at Hall and Company, they pulled off a job on Bowery!

For that miscue, Sergeant Fennelly was called on the carpet.

"Well," said the irate Commissioner, "You've made us look like fools! You've kept fifteen men out all night on a wild goose chase, while Blackie pulls a job miles from where you're waiting for him."

"We set our trap too soon, that's all," defended Fennelly.

"Fennelly, it seems to me your ideas aren't working out so well. We haven't enough policemen on the force to keep every loft building covered day and night. I've just this to say: I want some results. You've had time to show more than you've done. I want results—in a hurry, Fennelly, or I'll have to make a change. That's all."

[74]

Presently one of Fennelly's men reported that Blackie had bought some brushes and gold paint.

"Gold paint?" ejaculated Fennelly. "Now I know they're ready for that Hall and Company job. Gold paint spoils fast. They got to use it quick. Remember that black oil cloth they bought. They're going to paint that to look like the front of the vault; then use it for a curtain and work behind it!"

So Fennelly set his trap again. Monk climbed up the water tank on the roof next door, then let down a rope ladder so the yeggs could get on the roof. In no time at all they had the safe open, taking nothing but gold and platinum at Blackie's orders—seventy-five or maybe a hundred grand, according to their gloating estimations.

But around the building waited Fennelly's men. "Let's go down into the basement of this building," suggested Fennelly, "start the sidewalk elevator, and that will start the elevator bell ringing. If I know Blackie, he will jump a foot. To him it will mean just one thing—a burglar alarm. Now," he directed his man, "start that elevator."

Then things began to happen! "Here they come, men!" shouted Fennelly, as shrill blasts of police whistles cut through the air. "After 'em!"

For a few minutes there was excitement enough, shots, cries: "Stop, or I'll shoot!" "Throw up your hands!" "Try and get me, Copper!" "Drop that gun!" "Look out!" "Get that guy."

"Look out for that girl," yelled one of the coppers. "The Monk's holding her in front of him. I'll get him."

Two shots followed, and then a yell: "Don't shoot! Don't shoot. I quit!"

"You better quit," snapped Fennelly to Blackie, "or you'll get what your two pals have got—over there! Keep those hands reaching!"

"Here's the Monk, Fennelly," said one of the cops.

"How about that girl, Martin—she hurt?"

"No, just scared when Monk tried to use her for a shield. She jerked away. Then I got him."

"Any of our boys hurt?"

"No, sir. All okay, and the mob cleaned up!"

"Yea," said Fennelly, "I see Bartelsky and Moscovitz are through. Better get a morgue wagon for them and bring our squad cars around." Turning to Blackie he added, "Well, Blackie, too bad that bell had to ring. Might have avoided shooting your pals, otherwise."

"Say," said the criminal, "where did that bug alarm come from? I figured we had 'em all fixed!"

"That wasn't any bug alarm, Blackie!" explained Fennelly. "That was just the warning bell on the sidewalk elevator in front of the restaurant over there. They were bringing up a load of garbage!"

"Well, I'll be . . ."

"The bell brought out our load sooner than we expected, that's all." As the squad cars arrived, Fennelly directed, "All right, you two . . . into the car!"

When Fennelly was called before the Commissioner this time he was told: "Fennelly, I've had a stream of business men's delegations in here again! Only this time, they want to commend you for your great work—breaking up those burglar gangs. And you've received a citation from the police honor board and been recommended for promotion!"

Out of his years of service among New York's 19,000 policemen, Captain Fennelly has this word to offer to young men: "In the twenty-eight years I have served on the police force, thousands of criminals have passed before me. I can tell you now that every hour of the criminal's life is an unhappy hour; that there is nothing to look forward to except a grave. If there is anyone who has thought of following a criminal career, drop it now, and with it your criminal friends, and tomorrow morning lift your chin up, walk out and face the world and make a place for yourself that will make you and your family proud."

Captain Fennelly's belief in intelligent police work, his untiring effort in bringing scientific detection into play against safe-breakers have reduced crime and saved property. Captain Fennelly conquered the handicaps of poverty and schooling and by his great work made New York City an unsafe place for safe-crackers.

A little woman found a brooch upon the street one day;
It looked to her like jewelry the 10-cent stores display.
She took it home to pin her waist while out to wash she
    went,
And day by day that trinket gleamed as o'er the tub she
    bent;

[77]

But no one stopped to notice it. No mistress at the door
Would cast a second glance at things the washerwoman
    wore.

"It is a pretty brooch," she thought. "I'll wear it while
    I may,
Then give it to my daughter on her graduation day.
It's rather sad to look at now; I've lost a pearl or two,
But I can pay a jeweler to make it good as new."
So when the happy time arrived she asked a man the cost
Of two small pearls which would replace the ones that
    she had lost.

The jeweler the trinket took and gravely looked it o'er.
Said he: "Wait just a moment, please; I fear 'twill cost
    you more
Than you expect. These pearls are rare." She trembled
    at his speech.
"For gems like this we'll have to charge two thousand
    dollars each.
This is a most expensive brooch, exquisite, charming,
    quaint!"
The washerwoman heard no more. She'd fallen in a faint.

To find that brooch police had searched the city up and
    down,
And all the time it glistened on a woman's gingham gown,
And all the time it glistened as she toiled some floor to
    scrub

Or shed its rays of loveliness above the steaming tub.
But like this washerwoman, countless folks, year in, year
    out,
Perhaps are blessed with riches they have never learned
    about.

                —*Tale of a Brooch*

MOTHER AND THE BABY

Mother and the baby! Oh, I know no lovelier pair,
For all the dreams of all the world are hovering 'round
    them there;
And be the baby in his cot or nestling in her arms,
The picture they present is one with never-fading charms.

Mother and the baby—and the mother's eye aglow
With joys that only mothers see and only mothers know!
And here is all there is to strife and all there is to fame,
And all that men have struggled for since first a baby
    came.

I never see this lovely pair nor hear the mother sing
The lullabies of babyhood, but I start wondering
How much of every man today the world thinks wise
    or brave
Is of the songs his mother sang and of the strength she
    gave.

"Just like a mother!" Oh, to be so tender and so true,

No man has reached so high a plane with all he's dared
to do.
And yet, I think she understands, with every step she
takes
And every care that she bestows, it is the man she makes.

Mother and the baby! And in fancy I can see
Her life being given gladly to the man that is to be,
And from her strength and sacrifice and from her
lullabies,
She dreams and hopes and nightly prays a strong man
shall arise.

BLOWING OUT OIL WELL FIRES

"Extry! Extry paper! Ten killed in oil well fire! Extry paper! Big oil well explosion! Extry!"

Blazing oil well fires, belching forth millions of dollars in wasted oil, their angry tongues of liquid flame reducing vast treasures of rich oil deposits to black smoke. For years such fires have raged on unchecked. Could they ever be stopped? Would some fearless engineer some day find a way to snuff out these billion dollar conflagrations?

On April 28, 1931 in the East Texas oil field near the town of Gladewater, the Cole No. 1 Well was flowing wild, sending streams of liquid gold high into the air. Drenched by the geyser of oil, a drilling crew labored on the rig seeking to cap the well. Near the derrick stood Glenn Harroun, Field Superintendent, talking to one of the drillers about the record gusher of 30,000 barrels a day, when there were sudden frantic cries of: "Fire! Fire!" "Jump." "Help!" In a moment the whole area was a blazing inferno.

Amid the frantic scenes a man informed Harroun, "There's only one fellow can put it out. That's Myron Kinley over in Tulsa—Myron and his brother Floyd!"

At the moment Myron and Floyd were just discussing the new oil journal, which had come in the mail with a story about the Rumanian gas well, which had been burning for two years.

"I tell you, Floyd," said Myron, "I could put that fire out if the Rumanian government would only give me a chance."

"Why talk about it?" replied Floyd. "They turned you down for the job when you went over there two years ago."

At that moment the telephone rang, and Myron answered, "Yes, this is Myron Kinley. . . Yes, Glenn. What's that? The well at Gladewater? We'll fly over right away. Be there in a couple of hours. Sure, we'll put 'er out." Turning to Floyd, he said, "Floyd, that was Glenn Harroun from Gladewater. The Cole No. 1 has blown up. Killed nine men. And still blazing like fury."

"The Cole No. 1!"

"Get busy, pack up our asbestos suits and load of nitroglycerine. I'll call the airport and tell 'em to get our plane warmed up."

In two hours the Kinley brothers were at the scene of one of the worst oil well fires in history.

"We got the water pumps, tractors, winches, all the machinery ready to fight the fire," reported Glenn Harroun.

"Great," replied Myron Kinley. "But first, we got to clear all the burning debris and hot metal from around the well, so they can't touch off any oil. Here, you men with the tractors. Pull out those burning tree stumps all around here. Get moving."

Floyd and Myron jumped into their asbestos suits and went into the flames to hook cables around the hot pipe and junk next to the fire. When they signaled, the men on the winches would drag the debris out.

"Now, you roustabouts with those hose lines!" directed Myron. "Keep behind those iron shields and play plenty of water on Floyd and me. Get as close to us and the fire as you can! You got to keep our asbestos suits drenched with water so we won't fry."

With that the Kinley brothers walked into the flaming furnace and systematically began their work of fastening cables to debris. Suddenly, however, a beam fell and pinned Myron to the ground, right in the fire. Floyd rushed over to help him, but the beam was too heavy for him to lift alone. By now their asbestos suits were steaming. Then a sergeant of the Texas Rangers rushed in and helped extricate Myron.

Out of the flames, the asbestos suits were ripped off, and it was found that Floyd and the sergeant were unharmed, but Myron had sustained a broken leg. It was eight days later, before Floyd was ready to shoot the blaze with nitrogelatin. When the big explosion came, it was as Floyd explained: "just like puffing out a candle!"

With that job successfully accomplished the Kinleys went home. Myron made up his mind that he was going to Rumania just as soon as his leg was healed. Myron M. Kinley went to Rumania and for a second time sought permission to extinguish a burning gas well there, a well that had blazed for over two years, defying all efforts of European engineers and scientists.

Obtaining an audience with the Rumanian minister of

industry, he was received in the Rumanian capital of Bucharest. "Fourteen men have lost their lives trying to put out that fire in the Moreni field," he was told. Why do you think you can put out the blaze, when our own engineers and experts have failed?"

"Your excellency, I'm not concerned with the failures of others," said Myron. "It's my own success that interests me. I promise you not a life will be lost if I'm given the job. You've spent hundreds of thousands of dollars trying to stop that fire, and the gas that has been going up in smoke and flame—that's been a loss of nearly $2,000,000 to the company, hasn't it?"

"That is approximately correct."

"Here's my proposition. Give me a contract to put out that fire and put the well under control. If I do it, you pay my fee. If I don't I get nothing."

"Hmm. That is worth considering. But it is suicide—suicide."

Receiving the consent from the minister on the grounds that he would take only two men into the huge crater two hundred and fifty feet across by sixty-five feet deep, Myron selected Grady Shoop, the field superintendent, who was an American and a gang-pusher.

Arriving at the field, he saw that all the old machinery had to be hauled out of the pit, along with all the old chain and cable and pipe. All around the hole were little flames burning where the gas seeped up through the roasted sand. Myron proposed to extinguish these by packing the crevices with cement and mud.

In a week or so, Myron was ready to demonstrate that he could snuff the blaze, at least momentarily, with an explosion of nitroglycerin and gelatin. When ready, he invited in the local engineers and the minister of industry to watch.

"Now, your excellency and gentlemen," he explained, "if you'll stand back, I'll explain this rig to you. This trolley, as you see, runs across the well pit and over the mouth of the well. Suspended from the trolley, you see this cartridge. It's an old drum, packed with gelatinized nitroglycerin—fifty kilograms. There is a detonator in the drum, connected by wire with this plunger here on the edge of the pit. Now, I'm going to send this drum along the trolley until it's over the well. Watch . . . Here she goes!"

Instantly there was a great explosion, followed by cries of: "It's out. The fire's out. It's amazing. A miracle. A miracle."

But in a moment, this excitement was dampened by the observations: "Mr. Kinley, the gas is burning again."

"I expected the gas would re-ignite," said Myron, "from some of these small fires around the crater. I just wanted to show you."

"Mr. Kinley," sternly reprimanded the minister, "you endangered the lives of myself and my associates by setting off that explosion, to accomplish nothing!"

"But I merely demonstrated."

"You demonstrated nothing but the danger in your methods, sir. My engineers inform me that your explosion

[85]

has shattered windows in the homes of people in the near-by villages. I therefore find it necessary now to forbid you to use any explosives without first obtaining the approval of my engineers!"

Naturally the Rumanian engineers were envious and made it impossible for Kinley to blow the fire out with nitro. But he did not give up. "Then we'll put it out some other way," he said to Grady Shoop. "I've blistered my hands and face from this fire. I've almost been smothered to death by cave-ins, and that's the way they appreciate it. Well, Grady, if they won't let us do it one way, we'll do it another. We'll stop off the gas supply, divert it through one of those old tunnels they built themselves. And I'll lick this job if it takes six months to do it."

And it was almost six months later that Mrs. Kinley back in Tulsa received a cablegram from Rumania informing her that he had put out the Moreni Well fire, had the well under control and was on his way home. After six months of persevering, heartbreaking labor, hindered at every turn by envy and red tape in the Rumanian government, he had achieved the feat. He made a 7000-mile run to put out a fire that had burned for two years and eight months, shooting a flame 250 feet high that roared on for 970 days. By his foresight, his ingenuity, his perseverance, Myron Kinley has conserved millions in natural resources.

I wonder what the world beyond can hold of beauty to
compare

With tulips gay in early May and trees in blossom everywhere.

Has God some loveliness retained of bloom and bird for
heaven alone,

Or is the fullness of His power to doubting man already
shown?

I know beyond the bonds of flesh the souls of men from
strife are free;

That life is ampler over there, but can the springtime
lovelier be?

Can breezes sweeter fragrance bear and daffodils more
perfect grow?

Can hills and fields more splendors wear than these we
common mortals know?

The Spring must be eternal, too. That burst of music
in the sky

Which sings the cardinal's joy of life I cannot think was
born to die.

I'm sure when robins nest again and beauty blossoms
everywhere,

Whatever else God's Heaven may hold, the Spring can be
no lovelier there.

—Eternal Spring

THE BOY'S IDEAL

I must be fit for a child to play with,
Fit for a youngster to walk away with;
  Fit for his trust and fit to be
  Ready to take him upon my knee;
Whether I win or I lose my fight,
I must be fit for my boy at night.

I must be fit for a child to come to,
Speech there is that I must be dumb to;
  I must be fit for his eyes to see,
  He must find nothing of shame in me;
Whatever I make of myself, I must
Square to my boy's unfaltering trust.

I must be fit for a child to follow,
Scorning the places where loose men wallow;
  Knowing how much he shall learn from me,
  I must be fair as I'd have him be;
I must come home to him, day by day,
Clean as the morning I went away.

I must be fit for a child's glad greeting,
His are eyes that there is no cheating;
  He must behold me in every test,
  Not at my worst, but my very best;
He must be proud when my life is done
To have men know that he is my son.

"SMART" PUBLISHER

THIS is the story of a man whose life has been a succession of doing, in the eyes of all who watched him, the wrong thing at the wrong time. Yet, today, just on the verge of forty, David A. Smart has accomplished the impossible, has written a new chapter in the history of the publishing business.

As a boy, Dave Smart had to work to earn the money to go to the circus and other shows with his childhood friends. From that beginning he early developed a belief in his ability to do things. He continued to believe that he could accomplish the impossible when at the ripe age of twelve he secured employment in a hat store. Soon he was top salesman in the shop, and soon he was out of a job. The shop had been holding a selling-out sale, and Dave Smart had literally worked himself out of a job!

Undaunted, the courageous boy went on to other jobs. A few years later, still in knee-pants he took a job in a Chicago newspaper office as a stenographer. Although he didn't know how to typewrite, he told his boss, "But I could learn, sir." From the typewriter in the classified department of the newspaper, he graduated to the sales department. There, on a commission basis, he developed a new selling technique and soon was earning $95 a week. Then one day he was called into the manager's office.

"Smart," said the manager, "I sent for you because I've got good news for you."

"Thank you, sir," said Dave politely.

"I've noticed the record you've hung up selling classified advertising on a commission basis. Well, you've made a name for yourself, boy, and I'm going to promote you to a regular selling job. Yes sir-ee, beginning next week, you're on a straight salary."

"Straight salary?"

"Yes, Smart. Beginning next Monday, you'll make $28 a week!"

And once again David Smart's success brought him failure, once again the master salesman sold himself out of a good job into a poor one. Still not discouraged, David Smart made new plans for his future. Then America called for volunteers. The great war was on, and Dave Smart followed his country's colors to France.

The war over, David Smart came back home, wounded, but the same courageous spirit that had carried him through his boyhood days, carried him through the first years of the depression. Dave Smart had found his way into the publishing business. Making a modest start, with the same meager capital and experience he had drawn upon before, he kept his business going and growing, while competitors fought desperately to keep their businesses alive.

At a conference with his brother, Alfred, and a friend in his office he was told, "But Dave, can't you realize we're in a depression. You can't bring out a new magazine now."

"Listen, Dave," said another adviser. "A fifty-cent

magazine is impossible. Why, there have been a dozen magazine failures during this depression. Have you read the papers? Have you heard of the proposed bank holiday? The President may act."

To all this, Dave Smart replied, "We're going to publish this new magazine, depression or no depression, and it's going to sell for fifty cents. Look, have you ever seen a man's magazine that looked like this? Have you ever seen illustrations that compared with these? We're going on the news stands, and this dummy is going to the printer."

To the printer went David Smart, and with him went the dummy of his new fifty-cent magazine. Business failures brought on by the depression, threatened bank holiday, nothing could stop him. He went to the office of a large news distributing company.

"This, then, is the dummy copy of your new magazine, Mr. Smart?"

"That's ESQUIRE."

"And you propose to ask fifty cents a copy for this publication?"

"Exactly. And having acquainted you with our plans, I'd like to supply you with 50,000 copies of the first number to be put on the news stands throughout the country. You see . . . "

"I don't want to dampen your enthusiasm for the publication, Mr. Smart," said the distributor, "but I'm afraid that . . . "

"Afraid?"

"Yes, I'm afraid you're over-enthusiastic. After all our years of experience, well, if you are 100% successful with your new venture, you may hope to sell 19,000 copies. That would mean you would have to print 25,000 copies."

"You may be right in your figures," conceded Smart. "But I'm willing to take the risk. I'll ship you 25,000 copies of ESQUIRE as soon as they're off the press."

And to the news distributing company went 25,000 copies of ESQUIRE. Soon there was a call for 25,000 more! Smart was able to supply them, because he had printed 100,000! Day by day there were calls for 5,000 . . . 10,000.

The acceptance of ESQUIRE was sensational. News stands were besieged. Even David Smart's belief in his new magazine, a belief that prompted him to have 100,000 copies printed, was not sufficient to meet the demand. Today, ESQUIRE monthly sells around 600,000 copies, and David Smart's newest contributions to the magazine readers of America, CORONET and KEN, are equally sensational in their success, circulation and prosperity.

In explanation of the phenomenal way in which his periodicals have "caught on," Mr. Smart says, "I guess it gets down to the good old philosophy of giving people more than they expect to get for their money." And that is a natural philosophy to Dave Smart, for he says that the biggest kick he gets out of his brilliant success at the age of forty "is to see others come along in my business and find outstanding success. I have had the very great pleasure of seeing several of my associates become wealthy in my business."

Life is a struggle for peace,
  A longing for rest,
A hope for the battles to cease,
  A dream for the best;
And he is not living who stays
  Contented with things,
Unconcerned with the work of the days
  And all that it brings.

He is dead who sees nothing to change,
  No wrong to make right;
Who travels no new way or strange
  In search of the light;
Who never sets out for a goal
  That he sees from afar
But contents his indifferent soul
  With things as they are.

Life isn't rest—it is toil;
  It is building a dream;
It is tilling a parcel of soil
  Or bridging a stream;
It's pursuing the light of a star
  That but dimly we see,
And in wresting from things as they are
  The joy that should be.

                              —*The Struggle*

JUST HALF OF THAT, PLEASE

Grandmother says when I pass her the cake:
  "Just half of that, please."
If I serve her the tenderest portion of steak:
  "Just half of that, please."
And be the dessert a rice pudding or pie,
As I pass Grandma's share she is sure to reply,
With the trace of a twinkle to light up her eye:
  "Just half of that, please."

I've cut down her portions but still she tells me:
  "Just half of that, please."
Though scarcely a mouthful of food she can see:
  "Just half of that, please."
If I pass her the chocolates she breaks one in two,
There's nothing so small but a smaller will do,
And she says, perhaps fearing she's taking from you:
  "Just half of that, please."

When at last Grandma leaves us the angels will hear:
  "Just half of that, please."
When with joys for the gentle and brave they appear:
  "Just half of that, please."
And for fear they may think she is selfish up there,
Or is taking what may be a young angel's share,
She will say with the loveliest smile she can wear:
  "Just half of that, please."

[94]

FIRST LADY OF THE BATON

THE bravos of the galleries in the concert hall! The plaudits of the music patrons and critics in the boxes! The thrill of artistic achievement with the symphony baton—reached only after years of struggle and self-denial! Success attained only by hurdling the age-old obstacle of prejudice against a woman in a professional career. That is the true life story of America's first lady of the baton, Ebba Sundstrom, Conductor of the Woman's Symphony Orchestra of Chicago and the first American-born woman to conduct a symphony.

The story of Ebba Sundstrom has its beginning in the small midwestern town of Lindsborg, Kansas, home of the famous Bethany Oratorio Society. On her seventh birthday there, a little blue-eyed, blond-curled Ebba was gayly surprised by the gift of a small-sized violin from her brother Carl. "Now," she exulted, "I won't have to use your big violin to practice on any more."

At the age of twelve the little girl was playing in the Oratorio orchestra, and at that age actually teaching the violin to other little girls of the town. Then there was bad news one day, as her father, a carpenter, decided that the family must move to McAlester, Oklahoma, where there was a building boom. "Your brother, Carl," he explained to Ebba, "is going away to teach school at Monmouth College in Illinois, and your sister, Ella, is going to Minneapolis to work and study with your other sister, Myrtle. So, Ebba, you and the other children, I'm taking you where I can get work to support you."

Some months later Carl returned home on a visit. There he found Ebba quite busy leading a string trio at the hotel during dinner time and in the evening playing with the theater orchestra. But she was not happy. She worked hard, but she was not happy because there was no chance for her to study music. Then it was that Carl suggested that she return with him to Monmouth, where there was a school orchestra.

After a demonstration on her violin, Ebba convinced the music professor of the school that she belonged in his orchestra, although previously women had been excluded. Soon, however, she received a letter from her sister Ella in Minneapolis, saying, "Myrtle and I are happy to hear how well you've done at Monmouth. But now, we want you to come and live with us in Minneapolis. We've arranged for you to study at the Minneapolis School of Music, under Richard Czerwonky, the Conductor of the Minneapolis Symphony."

At Minneapolis, Ebba substituted as leader of the choir when her sister Myrtle became ill, and one evening she walked home from church with Victor Nylander. "It took me a long time to get you to pay some attention to the leading tenor in the choir," said he, laughing.

"I know, Victor," answered Ebba. "But since my sisters brought me to Minneapolis eight years ago, I've been so occupied with my music that I've had little time."

"Ebba, dear," he said, "do you think some day I could

IT CAN BE DONE

crowd into your thoughts—along with your dreams of a
great musical career?"

"Victor, darling," she replied, "there's no need for me
to crowd you in. You know I've thought of you a lot,
since we met, but I still hope some day . . . "

"To be a great musician. And some day you *will* be,
Ebba. But do you think some day, you might also become . . . Mrs. Victor Nylander?"

"Some day, Victor, dear . . . but not right now, *especially* not right now."

"And why especially not *now?*"

"Mr. Czerwonky has been invited to Chicago as head
of the violin department of Bush Conservatory. He's
asked me to go along as his assistant."

"And you've decided to go?"

"Yes, I have, Victor. I hate to leave you, but it will
be a great opportunity for me."

"Of course, Ebba. I'll have to wait. That's all."

"I'm sorry, Victor."

"We'll be apart for a while, Ebba," said Victor. "But
I won't let you stay away from me long. As soon as I
can complete my work here, I'll follow you to Chicago."

"And I'll be waiting for you, dear," she promised.

Two years later Victor *did* follow her to Chicago.
"Ebba, darling," he told her. "I've come to Chicago to
stay."

"Victor, how grand! I've missed you so much."

"And I missed you, too, Ebba. How have you been
getting along?"

"It was quite a struggle at first," she explained, "to build up my classes at the conservatory and to keep myself going. I had to find engagements outside, substituting for theater organists, playing at club concerts, for churches. It was an awful grind. But I didn't mind it."

"Well, darling, that's all over now. Are you ready to become Mrs. Nylander?"

"Yes."

At that moment in marched Czerwonky, "Miss Sundstrom, oh, I beg your pardon. I . . . I thought you were alone. I'm sorry."

"Oh, come in, Mr. Czerwonky," said Ebba. "I want you to meet my fiance—Dr. Victor Nylander."

"How do you do, how do you do!" said Czerwonky. "Your fiance?"

"That's right," inserted Victor. "We're going to be married just as soon as . . . "

"Oh, my, that's bad news, bad news indeed," replied Czerwonky. "I mean, well, I was just going to discuss some plans with Miss Sundstrom, plans for a woman's symphony orchestra."

"A woman's symphony orchestra?" exclaimed Ebba.

"Yes, and I wanted you to be concertmeister. But now, you'll be going away."

"Ebba," Victor took up the conversation again, "I don't see any reason why you can't become a concertmeister even if we are married."

"Oh, Victor," she showered him enthusiastically. "You, you're grand."

"Good, good," commented Czerwonky. "Then we shall make plans and arrange for a rehearsal at once."

It was at one of the rehearsals that Czerwonky said, "Now, ladies . . . please! A little more vigor, please . . . when you play. I know you are ladies, but remember, you are supposed to be musicians—musicians! A symphony! Here, Miss Sundstrom . . . "

"Yes, Mr. Czerwonky?"

"Here, you take this baton, and now you conduct."

"But Mr. Czerwonky!"

"You conduct, I say. I want to go to the back of the room and hear how it sounds."

"But I don't know, what do I do? What do I do, with my left hand?"

"Your left hand? Why, use it to conduct with. What do you suppose?"

"But I've never, I've never . . . Mr. Czerwonky, these women musicians, why, they'll never pay attention to a woman leader. I . . . I can't . . . "

"Then, you think you cannot conduct? You are afraid?"

"No, I'm not afraid! I *can* do it."

"Good. I've been planning to make you the regular conductor. Now, go ahead, conduct, Miss Sundstrom, conduct!"

At the Century of Progress in Chicago, the Woman's Symphony Orchestra conducted by Ebba Sundstrom was one of the features of the great show. The concerts of the eighty-piece orchestra were acclaimed alike by the public and the critics. And by this time, Ebba Sundstrom also

[99]

was teaching music to her own small son, Reinhold.

A great musician and a great mother; that is the story of Ebba Sundstrom. Through her talent and leadership, she brought the Woman's Symphony of Chicago into national recognition as one of the top symphonic organizations in the nation!

The world of music is to me
　An ancient country far away
Which I am not allowed to see,
　Beyond its borders I must stay.
Still, as a boy who looks at ships
　And pictures of some distant land,
The wish is ever on my lips
　That some day I may understand
And some day go at last to share
The ecstasy that must be there.

I hear them talk who know it well
　About the golden hours of song.
I listen as its people tell
　Of wood wind notes a half-tone wrong,
But as the orchestra begins
　A most majestic symphony
The magic of the violins
　No inner meaning brings to me.
I cannot pass the citadels
To tread the path where music dwells.

I envy them who walk its ways
  And claim the joys denied to me,
I know it is a realm ablaze
  With beauty I shall never see.
I'd like to walk its shores alone
  And feel my soul with rapture swept,
But I was fashioned deaf to tone,
  So at the outer wall I'm kept.
Friends freely pass within the gate
And leave me in the cold to wait.
                        —*The World of Music*

EXAMPLE

Perhaps the victory shall not come to me,
  Perhaps I shall not reach the goal I seek.
  It may be at the last I shall be weak
And falter as the promised land I see;
Yet I must try for it and strive to be
  All that a conquerer is. On to the peak,
Must be my call—this way lies victory!
  Boy, take my hand and hear me when I speak.

There is the goal. In honor make the fight.
  I may not reach it but, my boy, you can.
Cling to your faith and work with all your might,
  Some day the world shall hail you as a man.
And when at last shall come your happy day,
Enough for me that I have shown the way.

SERVICE

I have no wealth of gold to give away,
   But I can pledge to worthy causes these:
   I'll give my strength, my days and hours of ease,
My finest thought and courage when I may,
And take some deed accomplished for my pay.
   I cannot offer much in silver fees,
But I can serve when richer persons play,
   And with my presence fill some vacancies.

There are some things beyond the gift of gold,
   A richer treasure's needed now and then;
Some joys life needs which are not bought and sold—
   The high occasion often calls for men.
Some for release from service give their pelf,
But he gives most who freely gives himself.

AUTO CAMPER

THE "Covered Wagon" of the past, historical conveyance of America's pioneers—crude, rough, lumbering, plodding forward toward new horizons—little realized that it was the forerunner of the "Covered Wagon" of today—sleek, smart and well-appointed automobile trailer, the modern-day conveyance of America's new pioneers.

Arthur G. Sherman, forty-six, is by profession a bacteriologist, by hobby, a camper . . . by chance, inventor and builder of "Covered Wagon" automobile trailers. His is the story of a man who was successful in his chosen field and then turned his energies toward a new endeavor, toward an uncharted industry.

The son of Dr. G. H. Sherman, Arthur Sherman embarked on his career as a bacteriologist in 1911. He worked long and hard developing vaccines to be used in fighting colds, pneumonia and whooping cough. In 1926 Mr. Sherman was completing an important bit of research in his laboratory. He removed the slide from his microscope and straightened up from his work-bench.

"Ah, well," he sighed. "That's that!"

"Completed, chief?" asked his assistant.

"Completed. The experiment is done. And I'm nearly done, too."

"We need a rest, Mr. Sherman. You've been working too hard. What you ought to do is take a vacation."

"By golly," said Sherman, "that's just what I *will* do!

I'll pack mother and the kids, all five of 'em, into the car and we'll take ourselves a trip!"

At home, Mr. Sherman said to his wife, "Now, dear, it's like this. You see, I thought that maybe this year we could really see a bit of the country . . . I saw it on my way back from the laboratory today. It's a trailer. It hitches right on to the back of the car, and it has a tent in it. Takes just ten minutes to put it up, and you've got your own home. Can you imagine taking your vacation with your own home on wheels?"

So Sherman bought one of the trailers and set out on his trip. But unfortunately the new-fangled contraption did not work as easily as the salesman had promised and predicted. After wrestling with the tent a good deal longer than the allotted ten minutes, Sherman exclaimed in exasperation, "I'm going to put up this tent if it kills me, and when we get back home I'm going to build a real trailer—one that people can live in without being architectural engineers!"

Back home he employed a cabinet maker and together they set to work constructing a real trailer in Sherman's garage. It was a trailer that one did not have to take apart every night and fold up—nine feet long, its bottom dropped right down when ready to camp.

While his children were giving it the critical "once over," Sherman happened to think, "We haven't named it. Come on, children. What'll we call it?"

"Well, Dad," remarked one of the boys. "It looks just like the covered wagon!"

"It sure does," said another.

"That's it," agreed Sherman. "That's just the name for it. We'll call it 'The Covered Wagon.' "

And it was from just that humble beginning that the modern Covered Wagon Trailer sprang. In the summer of 1928, Arthur Sherman and his family bravely set out to blaze trails with their Covered Wagon. It was at first a curiosity. People stopped to look and to ask questions.

"That's quite a contraption you got there, mister," they said.

"Yeah, slick way of takin' the family on a vacation, I'd say."

"Oh, I think it's cunning! I must have John get one for us. Where did you buy yours?"

"I made this one," explained Sherman. "That is, I designed it myself. But I wouldn't be surprised if some one of these days you couldn't go right into a store and buy one."

When Sherman first thought of manufacturing the trailers himself for sale, he was told it was a "crazy idea," but he retorted, "It's no crazier than the idea behind the first automobile or the electric refrigerator or any other one of a thousand modern conveniences we have come to accept."

In 1929 Arthur G. Sherman made one hundred Covered Wagon Trailers and sold them. He invested $10,000 in his belief that the modern pioneers of America were ready for the modern-day "covered wagon." Today that $10,000 investment has grown into a $10,000,000 business. Today throughout America on highways and by-ways alike, the automobile trailer provides a healthful, inexpensive, fun-giving conveyance for both rich and poor.

At Mount Clemens, Michigan, the Covered Wagon Company, employing more than 14,000 men, sends forth more than eighty trailers a day. Since the company was founded, Mr. Sherman estimates that they have turned out approximately 15,000 Covered Wagons. The trailers run in three different sizes, from sixteen feet to twenty-two feet in length over all and are equipped to accommodate four persons comfortably, though occasionally they are equipped to sleep six persons.

As Mr. Sherman explains, "We have complete, compact kitchenette with complete cooking facilities—ice box, kitchen sink, storage space for pots and pans and shelves for vegetables, groceries, etc. And, of course, we have a heating stove for winter, lavatory with provisions for a refreshing sponge bath, toilet, small dresser, vanity, writing desks and chairs and, of course, wardrobes for clothes. The floors are covered with linoleum or carpeting, if desired. We have insulated the new Covered Wagons with a new type aluminum foil in order to protect them against the heat and cold. This became necessary because many trailers were sold to construction engineers, geologists and people in like professions who are forced to be away from their home on the job and must have a place to live."

"The main advantage in traveling in a trailer," declares Mr. Sherman, "is that you can stop at places you couldn't get to on a train. You see, it is not so much the desire to beat the cost of traveling as it is to get a thrill out of this new method of traveling. As a matter of fact, many wealthy people are Covered Wagon owners. Gypsy Rose Lee, for example, has one of our trailers. Fred Stone is a trailer owner. Carveth Wells, the noted explorer, is another Covered Wagon owner, and there was a Covered Wagon shown in the Fibber McGee and Molly picture—'This Way Please.'"

Yes, the automobile trailer is now an established part of the great American plan of living, all because Arthur G. Sherman, a determined man with a far-seeing vision, believed that it could be done. Arthur Sherman believed that America was still the land of opportunity, that Americans still nurtured the spirit of the pioneer. Whether Arthur Sherman had toyed with the idea of a trailer or with any other idea, the net result would have been the same—success, the kind of success that any American can carve for himself once he throws his mind and heart to the task.

The road lay straight before him, but the bypaths smiled
  at him
And the scarlet poppies called him to the forests cool and
  dim,
And the song birds' happy chorus seemed to lure him further on;

[107]

'Twas a day of wondrous pleasure—but the day was
quickly gone.

He could not resist the laughter and the purling of a brook
Any more than gray old sages can resist some dusty book,
And though stern-faced duty bade him march the high-
way straight ahead,
"The trees are better company than busy men," he said.

We wondered at his dreaming and his wanderings far
astray,
But we were counting values by the gold and silver way,
And sometimes as I saw him gazing idly at the sky,
I fancied he had pleasures of a sort I couldn't buy.

I fancy he saw something in the clouds above the trees
Which the gold and glory seeker passes by and never sees,
And I think he gathered something from the woods and
running streams
Which is just as good as money to the man of many
dreams.

—*The Dreamer*

CURLICUES

FUNNY little marks on paper, queer curlicues made by rapidly moving pencils; these are the intriguing figures of the science popularly known as shorthand. Shorthand, the language of business, of law, of diplomacy—the language of nearly every human endeavor.

The man who is greatly responsible for the growth of modern shorthand, the man whose system of shorthand is used in nearly every English-speaking country, is Dr. John R. Gregg, another living example of the will to win. His true life story is further proof that with determination anything is possible.

Today, Dr. Gregg, a young man of sixty-nine is honored throughout the world as a leading educator, an outstanding business man, a publisher of the first rank. But in his life is written a most amazing story of the "will-to-do." John Gregg's career is truly an inspiration to every young American, for it points to the glory that is the reward of grit and determination.

Born in Ireland, Dr. Gregg even as a child was to meet with life's sometimes harsh treatment. In school he was backward. His teacher railed at him, "You should be ashamed of yourself. Your brother and sister are at the *head* of the class, while you—there doesn't even seem to be room for *you* at the foot!"

Then one day in class a boy whispered to him, "Watcha gonna do after school?"

"I dunno," answered John. "I think maybe I'll just go home and . . . "

"So," stormed the teacher, breaking in. "John Gregg! And you, Tom! Whispering! Against my express orders."

"Well, we were just . . . "

"Just 'putting your heads together,' eh? Well, suppose I just take hold of each of your heads and put them together . . . like *this!* Perhaps that will teach you that I'm not to be disobeyed!"

Later at home, John Gregg's sister asked him, "Did, did teacher hurt you much when she banged your head against Tom's?"

His brother spoke up, "Boy, I'll bet it hurt plenty. It was a sound crack, all right. Did it hurt?"

But there was no reply from the boy.

"Johnny!" repeated his sister. "We asked you something! Hey!"

"Huh?" replied John. "Did, did you say something to me?"

"Did we *say* something to you?" cried his brother. "Sister and I both just asked you if teacher hurt you much when she banged your head. Did she?"

"That's funny," said John slowly. "I . . . I can see . . . I can see your lips move, but I . . . I can't hear what you're saying!"

Thus did tragedy strike at John Robert Gregg when he was but a child. Already backward, he was further handicapped with the burden of deafness, brought on by his teacher's punishment! But John Gregg was not one to mope about his affliction. Heroically he struggled with his lessons, learning the hard way—through patient perusal of his studies hour upon hour.

Then one day came the circumstance which was to be the turning point of his life. His father brought home a book on shorthand used by his friend, Annesley, in taking down the minister's sermons at church. "I want you all to apply yourselves to it," he told his children. "I want you to learn to write like that. I'm figuring it will stand you in good stead some day, if you do."

John Gregg doggedly pursued his studies, tackling first one, then another and another until he had mastered, in theory only, the six systems of shorthand then in use. He was sixteen now, and his father had plans for his future!

"I don't care if you aren't interested in reading law," said his father. "I've made arrangements, and to Glasgow you'll go. There you'll read law; and if you read enough you'll be a lawyer."

But on the side, while being abused by a drunken and insolent master, John Gregg was busy figuring out a new idea about "Light Line Phonography." "I'm looking ahead, maybe twenty-five or thirty-five years," he explained to a friend, "when shorthand and stenography will revolutionize business. Why, I can see men and women at long rows of desks, working swiftly from shorthand notes. I can see business speeded up twice as fast, five times as fast as it is now."

When ready with his text, John went to his brother and asked for a loan of fifty dollars to publish his book and to open a school. Reluctantly his brother put up the money, and John Gregg, aged twenty-five, promptly advanced it to the printer for his text book.

In Liverpool, where his book was printed, with his last few remaining pennies, he opened his first school of shorthand. Five flights up, he found his quarters. But the pupils didn't find the five flights inviting, and the city of Liverpool was not ready to receive young Gregg and his "light-line phonography."

So, six years later, with a capital of $150, John Gregg, again beaten by life, turned his face toward new horizons. In Boston, he tried again. With but a handful of students and with but very little money, he closed the doors of his Boston school for the holidays, discovering that he had exactly forty cents! His school closed its doors for lack of capital and for lack of students, and John Robert Gregg, again defeated, headed west . . . to Chicago.

But what was his fortune in the Windy City but to run into a fire, in which his last worldly possessions vanished in smoke. And with this would have gone the last hopes of most people, but not John Robert Gregg! The iron will, the grit and determination that had seen him this far was to see him through once again.

From the smouldering ashes, Mr. Gregg began to rebuild his destroyed fortunes, and from those ashes have risen the splendid career of the educator whose system of shorthand is taught in ninety per cent of the public schools of America, whose memory is perpetuated every day as flying fingers trace the little symbols of speech, which, when translated, become the language of the world, the life-blood of commerce, industry and law.

Today the Gregg System of Shorthand is taught in thirteen different languages: French, German, Italian, Spanish, Portuguese, Russian, Polish, Chinese, Japanese, Irish and some others. Approximately a million and a half persons use it professionally, and the system is taught in 16,000 schools in America. Many great men have come up the ladder of success, starting as stenographers. Frank Vanderlip, former president of the National City Bank, started in Chicago as a stenographer. Calvin Gage was Secretary of Treasury under McKinley and then went on upward. Woodrow Wilson, John J. Raskob, Herbert Hoover—these were but a few of the outstanding personalities who used shorthand as a stepping stone to success.

When John Gregg arrived in Chicago he had seventy-five dollars, and although no one has even put five cents into the business, today it is a million and a half dollar business annually.

John Robert Gregg believed that it could be done, and because he believed, the world today moves faster, sends it messages more quickly, as it makes its funny little marks on paper, the marks of John Robert Gregg. He made possible a pleasant and profitable livelihood for thousands upon thousands of young men and women, and he brought speed and efficiency to business.

When you're up against a trouble,
  Meet it squarely, face to face;
Lift your chin and set your shoulders,
  Plant your feet and take a brace.
When it's vain to try to dodge it,
  Do the best that you can do;
You may fail, but you may conquer,
  See it through!

Black may be the clouds about you
  And your future may seem grim,
But don't let your nerve desert you;
  Keep yourself in fighting trim.
If the worst is bound to happen,
  Spite of all that you can do,
Running from it will not save you,
  See it through!

Even hope may seem but futile,
  When with troubles you're beset,
But remember you are facing
  Just what other men have met.
You may fail, but fall still fighting;
  Don't give up, whate'er you do;
Eyes front, head high to the finish.
  See it through!

—*See It Through*

OLD BALLAD

MEMORIES, memories of a rosy-cheeked little boy, a poor little boy, with a great love for music. Memories of a brave understanding mother, a mother who was determined that that poor little boy should realize his ambition. That is the story of Egbert Van Alstyne, one of America's beloved composers. It is a story by turns stirring and poignant, and it is written in the notes of some of the world's most popular songs.

Remember when you used to sing, "In the Shade of the Old Apple Tree"? Egbert Van Alstyne wrote that melody. It is one of the world's greatest tune hits, one that has lived down through the years. But let us go back to retrace the tortuous steps that marked his climb to fame, back to 1884 when Egbert Van Alstyne was six years old. In the "sitting" room of his parents' home at Rockford, Illinois he was waiting for the return of his mother.

When she entered the room he cried, "Oh, Mother! I'm so glad you've come home."

"That's sweet of you to say, dear," she laughed. "But, why . . ."

"Please, mom! Please pump this organ for me. Please. I know I can play that hymn Daddy was singing at church Sunday, but . . . but I can't reach the pedals!"

"Darling, of course I'll pump for you. Here, move over."

[115]

And presently as the tune began to exude from the instrument, the little boy exclaimed triumphantly, "See. I told you I could. Oh, Mother. When are we going to have a piano, and when can I start taking lessons?"

"Some day, we *will* have a piano," she promised him, "and some day you will be able to have lessons. But now . . . well, dear, we're poor, and we can't afford to. But don't you worry, we'll manage it somehow."

And there came the time when they *did* have a piano, a real piano. Old fashioned as it was, it was the most beautiful piano in the whole world to little Egbert Van Alstyne. However, his days of ecstasy were brief. Came the time when Egbert's step-father believed it necessary to move to Missouri to live in a log cabin. It would be impossible to take the piano, and Egbert would have to give up his piano lessons. The best they could do was to take along a small organ. "That will be almost as good, won't it, dear?" said his mother.

"Yes, Mother," limply and bravely agreed the boy. "That'll be . . . just great!"

Such was the underlying strain of Egbert Van Alstyne's boyhood, the sad melody of unrealized ambition, underscored with the somber notes of poverty. But the boy and his mother were determined to write a brighter tune.

At the age of thirteen Egbert received his first real musical instruction at Cornell College, Mount Vernon, Iowa. Then, moving forward another step, he went to Chicago. At the Chicago Musical College, he received a free scholarship from Dr. Ziegfeld.

"Thank you, Doctor Ziegfeld," he said on receiving the award. "I want you to know how much this means to me. I want to be a really good pianist."

"That's the spirit!" replied Dr. Ziegfeld. "And you can do it. Any young man can make good in this country. That's what I told my son, Florenz, the other day. You know, that young scamp has gone to New York. New York, mind you. He says he's going to make the name of Florenz Ziegfeld mean something in the theatrical business!"

Egbert Van Alstyne's first job was playing with a traveling show, a road show. They got as far as Nogales, New Mexico where the show broke down, and for a while the coming composer hammered the keys in a border saloon for his cakes. The patrons laughed at him, because it was reported around that he had said he was going to be a composer.

The arrangement of the score that was Egbert Van Alstyne's life had been changed, changed by necessity, but the underlying theme remained the same. Six months later, he was back in Chicago, back at the piano, while Harry Williams, who was to become his partner and collaborator, stood penciling a lyric at his side.

"Play that again," he directed. "From the fifth bar. There."

"Okay, Harry," replied Egbert, striking a few bars.

"That's it. Now I can finish this lyric, and then we're set for New York. We're going to take our numbers to Tin Pan Alley."[2]

Arriving in the metropolis with just $7.80 between them, they decided they'd better look for jobs the first thing. "I'll try Shapiro and Bernstein," said Van Alstyne, "and you try . . . "

At Shapiro and Bernstein's, Van Alstyne was greeted by the former with: "No, mine young friend, your songs I'm not looking at!"

"But, if you'll only . . . "

"Your songs," repeated Shapiro firmly, "I'm not looking at! But if you can play the piano like you say, playing our catalogue songs you can! It's a job. You play, and dot's all! Twelf dollars a week. And you start in da morning at eight!"

Then one day Shapiro came to Van Alstyne and Williams and said, "So, you two boys been wanting to write songs for a long time you're telling me. Vell, now comes it the chance! Marie Hale, de big musical comedy star, she's liking for a song about de vest! You know, where is it da cowboys and Indians! You boys lived dere, you say. So, go ahead and write it up a song!"

A few days later, Egbert reported to Shapiro: "Listen, we got it! We got the song for Marie Hale! Look! Here it is."

"So, already you got it, eh?" replied Shapiro skeptically. "H'mmm. Vot kind of nonsense is dis? Navy Joe? Is dot a name for a western song, Navy Joe?"

"It's Navajo. Navajo," corrected Van Alstyne. "That's the way they say it! The 'j' is pronounced like an 'h.' "

"Navy Joe, you should say it Navajo? Listen, boys.

Mit me it's no monkey business, I want. I know a little something about the west mineself. Ain't I been to Pittsboigh three times? If a void is 'na vaho' spell it mit a 'H.' Besides, I ain't even hoid it yet. An' in all probables it ain't even worth listening to!"

But "Navajo" *was* worth listening to. It marked the first rise in the ascendancy of Egbert Van Alstyne's star. Together with his collaborator, Harry Williams, at the old Bell Hotel on Twenty-second Street, the boy who was determined to be a success embarked on his career as a composer. One day in a room on the second floor back Van Alstyne exclaimed, "We got something, I tell you. It's just about time for an old-fashioned ballad to catch on."

"Bert's right," agreed Harry Williams. "This ballad we've written will be a sensation."

"It'll be a bust," predicted a friend who was present. "Look, boys, why waste your time on a ballad when nobody wants ballads, when nobody sings ballads?"

Nevertheless, some weeks later the manager of the Hammerstein Music Hall was announcing: "It is the pleasure of the management always to try to bring you the newest and finest in entertainment. And so tonight we bring you the newest song sensation in America: "In the Shade of the Old Apple Tree."

Soon all America was singing Egbert Van Alstyne's beautiful ballad. And all the world is still singing it. Up to 1927 over twenty-six million copies had been sold. The world had been given music that it could understand and love, by a young man who knew that it could be done.

[119]

But the score of Egbert Van Alstyne's success was just begun. Soon were to follow: "Won't You Come Over to My House," "Memories," "Pretty Baby," "That Old Gal of Mine," "Drifting and Dreaming" . . . more than 500 songs that singers everywhere have given to appreciative audiences.

Today, Egbert Van Alstyne at sixty years of age has just finished seven brand new songs that promise to be hits. His mother, the woman who believed in him, Mrs. Van Alstyne, beloved "Aunt Em" of the radio, is eighty-two.

And as twilight falls in his mother's home, Egbert Van Alstyne sits at the piano:

"That's nice, son. What's the name of it?"

"I don't know; it hasn't a name yet, Mother. You see, I was just sitting here at the piano thinking about a little boy and his mother . . . *and* a piano . . . "

You can talk about your music, and your operatic airs,
And your phonographic record that Caruso's tenor bears;
But there isn't any music that such wondrous joy can
     bring
Like the concert when the kiddies and their mother start
     to sing.

When the supper time is over, then the mother starts to
     play
Some simple little ditty, and our concert's under way.

And I'm happier and richer than a millionaire or king
When I listen to the kiddies and their mother as they sing.

There's a sweetness most appealing in the trilling of their
    notes;
It is innocence that's pouring from their little baby
    throats;
And I gaze at them enraptured, for my joy's a real thing
Every evening when the kiddies and their mother start
    to sing.

—Real Singing

WHEN THE YOUNG ARE GROWN

Once the house was lovely, but it's lonely here to-day,
For time has come an' stained its walls an' called the
    young away;
An' all that's left for mother an' for me till life is through
Is to sit an' tell each other what the children used to do.

We couldn't keep 'em always an' we knew it from the
    start;
We knew when they were babies that some day we'd
    have to part.
But the years go by so swiftly, an' the littlest one has
    flown,
An' there's only me an' mother now left here to live alone.

Oh, there's just one consolation, as we're sittin' here
    at night,

They've grown to men an' women, an' we brought 'em
    up all right;
We've watched 'em as we've loved 'em an' they're
    splendid, every one,
An' we feel the Lord won't blame us for the way our
    work was done.

They're clean, an' kind an' honest, an' the world respects
    'em, too;
That's the dream of parents always, an' our dreams have
    all come true.
So although the house is lonely an' sometimes our eyes
    grow wet,
We are proud of them an' happy an' we've nothing to
    regret.

THE BARNUM OF BUGDOM

STARTING over late in life is certainly not easy. It requires a courage that is not found in the average man. Yet Mr. Frank E. Austin of Hanover, New Hampshire did just that. Broke, but no sluggard, Mr. Austin, a professor of electrical engineering and out of a job, faced the future with the same courage that had carried him down through the years. Now in his sixty-fourth year, hail, hearty and healthy, Mr. Austin is ambitious to carry on the job, or the industry, he himself created.

"Now Martha, dear," gamely said Frank Austin when the "bad news" that became so prevalent a few years back finally came to him, "don't be discouraged. One of these days we'll be back on our feet."

"I hope you're right," she answered, "but, after all, we're not as young as we once were."

"You know, Martha," said Frank, "I've always said a man is no older than he feels. I've got some useful years before me yet." Then he suddenly asked, "What did you do with the jar of ants I brought home last night?"

"Why . . . why, I threw them out. You know I can't have ants in my kitchen."

"But Martha, they were in a glass jar."

"Glass jar or no glass jar, I can't and won't have live ants in my house."

"Well," conceded Frank Austin, "maybe I'm working

on the wrong track. Maybe people won't stand for ants in their homes."

"Have you lost your mind, Frank?" demanded his wife. "Whatever in the world has possessed you to become so friendly with ants?"

"Not bad companions, Martha, not bad companions," he insisted. "They're industrious and thrifty. Guess almost every one of us could take a profitable lesson from them."

A few days later Mr. Austin invited his wife to come down to his work room in the basement. "There it is," he pointed with pride. "What do you think of it?"

"Frank Austin," she exclaimed. "Now what in the world do you call that crazy contraption? Two panes of glass, some sand in between, and . . . Frank Austin, you get those ants out of here this very minute."

"Now, Martha, hold on a minute. This is my new ant palace, the only thing of its kind in the whole world."

"I should hope it *is*. But what a foolish waste of time."

"Martha," he insisted, "this is the beginning of better times for us. I'm going to build and sell these ant palaces, and I'm going to begin the new business tomorrow morning. I'm convinced folks are going to like watching ants at their work."

Thus opened up a new career for Frank E. Austin, The Barnum of Bugdom, the gentleman who will stage a grand show of anything that creeps or crawls. In his famous observational Bee Houses and in his Ant Palaces, Mr. Austin learns the habits of these insects. He has a steady show, with no trouble with sit-down strikes.

The nearest thing to a sit-down strike is the male ant. "He never does a stroke of work throughout his entire life," says Frank. "He wears his Sunday clothes all week long. It has often been said that he has no brains, but what he does have he certainly uses, because he lets the women do all the work."

Mr. Austin rewards each industrious ant with a share of pure, golden honey, which may be obtained every night in the bee house, which may be kept in the living room. The response that Mr. Austin has had in the thousands of families who have given his ant palaces a fine reception proves that he had a sound idea. "After all," he says, "success seldom comes single-handed."

Broke, out of a job and with little to look forward to in the future, Mr. Austin started all over in his sixtieth year and came through with flying colors.

I know not whether middle age can fight again to win.
'Tis possible that youth alone can stand the battle's din.
Perhaps man's courage fades with time and fifty is too
     late
To have to start a second bout with all the odds of fate.
But this I know: that man is lost, though young or old
     he be,
Who says: "I'm sure it's vain to try; that task's too hard
     for me."

Perhaps from silvered brows they turn and ask for
     younger men;

Perhaps to men of middle age they give no chance again.
But long ago was failure known, and history appears
An endless tale of men who rose to fame when old in
years.
One fact of life is sure and 'tis the weakling soonest dies,
And in the dust that man must stay who will not try to
rise.

Too old to start anew? Ah, no! While health and will
remain,
Time locks no door against the man who wants to start
again!
Though some from thinning brows may turn, by history
is it told,
Full many a fortune has been won by men the world
called old.
'Tis not our years that cut us down, but fear and failing
will,
And who has spirit for the fight may live to conquer still.

—Spirit

MOONLIGHT SCHOOLS

"READIN' 'n writin' 'n 'rithmetic, done to the tune of a hick'ry stick" so went the words of that childhood rhyme so dear to us all. Cora Wilson Stewart, founder of Kentucky's Moonlight Schools, is the woman who made reading and writing possible to thousands who could do neither. Educator, humanitarian and saint of America's many, many illiterates, Mrs. Stewart's life is the stirring narrative of a courageous woman, a woman who kindled the torch of literacy that its light might shine down on the underprivileged, uneducated masses who live in Kentucky's mountains. Enemy of ignorance, friend to the unlettered and unlearned, Cora Wilson Stewart proved that education could be brought to all, that knowledge could be disseminated by night as well as by day.

Back in 1911 in Rowan County, Kentucky where Cora Wilson Stewart was Superintendent of Schools, she was impressed by an old lady who had "larned" to read and write by sitting up night after night with a speller in order that she might be able to answer the letters from her daughter.

"How wonderful!" thought Mrs. Stewart. "If we could only teach everyone in Kentucky to do the same thing! The people *do* want to learn. It's only that they're unable to, unable because they can't attend day schools. Unable—because they're ashamed! But if we would give them the opportunity to attend *night* school . . . "

First she went to the teachers of Rowan County. "To-day," she said, "as you know, is Labor Day. It marks the beginning of our school terms. And what I'm asking you is not included in your agreement with the school term, nor with the school board. I am asking you to sacrifice your time, your evenings, to teaching the illiterate of Rowan County to read and write. Getting the older people to attend school at night will be a big job in itself. And teaching them the fundamentals of reading and writing will be an even greater task. Your reward, if any, will be in the happiness you will bring into the lives of these good, simple, honest people."

With the cooperation of her teachers, who were inspired by her, Cora Wilson Stewart went to the simple people of the Kentucky mountains on this mission of light, explaining, coaxing, begging the unlettered to join with them in the quest for primary knowledge. It was hard work, but Mrs. Stewart and her friends were not to be turned from the path they had chosen. The mountain folks walked from miles around to attend her Moonlight School. She pointed to words written on the blackboard, and they repeated them after her.

It was glorious indeed! For throughout Rowan County, the curtain of ignorance began to part, and the light of education to shine in upon those who had been long in darkness. And Cora Wilson Stewart began to cast her eyes toward other fields.

"We can do the same for the people of every other county in Kentucky," she said. "What was possible in

Rowan County is possible throughout the state. I'll not rest until all Kentucky, all of the United States is free from illiteracy!"

In 1914, his Excellency, James B. MacCreary, Governor of the Commonwealth of Kentucky appointed Mrs. Stewart a member of the State Illiteracy Commission. A few years later she dedicated her book, *The Soldier's First Reader*, to the men of Kentucky who had enlisted in the army to help the United States in the World War. She introduced education in the penitentiary, and in time Moonlight Schools were opened in Alabama, New York, Mississippi and other states.

Since that small beginning back in 1911, Mrs. Stewart has estimated that her Moonlight Schools have taught about two million people how to read and write. But she is not yet through, for there are still nearly three million people in the United States who are yet to be taught to read and write.

In teaching adult illiterates, the first problem is to teach them how to write their names. "There is no other copy," says Mrs. Stewart, "that will inspire them so much. We teach the student to write in grooves made in blotting paper, grooves like the grooves in the palm of my hand and yours, only much deeper. He takes the pencil and follows these grooved copies, some ten or twenty or more times, until he gets the form of his name and is able to leave the copies and write it on ordinary paper."

It usually takes only about thirty minutes of time to accomplish this much. In teaching a student to read,

[129]

Mrs. Stewart says, "We let him get acquainted with the sentence by speaking it before he sees it in print. He puts it in the form of a question to the teacher, 'Can you read?' Then he is shown the same sentence and asked to read it from the book. He next asks, 'Can you write?' Then, 'Can you read and write?' After each question, he is shown the sentence he has just spoken and reads it. This method of putting it as a question first, helps to wear off his embarrassment and to get naturalness of expression in reading. After each sentence in the lesson has been covered in this way, a drill is given on the words; then he reads the whole lesson. This occupies about a half an hour's time. It is our aim to teach an adult illiterate to write his name and to read a page in his book, in one hour's time. And only one dollar has been expended for each person who has been taught in our moonlight schools. It is a remarkably small expenditure, when you consider the good it does the person. It gives him a sense of power and he begins to boost and to cooperate with movements for community betterment and also, in many instances, to take leadership.

"Our work also extends into the homes to the teaching of individuals," Mrs. Stewart continues. "If one has a tenant on his farm, a laborer in his factory, a servant in his home, or a neighbor next door who cannot read or write, he will get to work, I hope, and teach him. We do not want the census taker on his rounds to find any illiterate mothers in this country in 1940, nor do we want him to find any illiterates anywhere. The time is approaching when the next census will list all who cannot read and write, and each community and state will take its rank for another decade. Our greatest task is just ahead—to wipe out illiteracy before the census of 1940."

Yes, Cora Wilson Stewart lighted the torch of knowledge down there in Rowan County, Kentucky way back in 1911. And the torch still burns bright throughout America! But Mrs. Stewart's work is not yet done. Each day she pushes farther and farther toward her goal on the horizon, a literate America. An America where truly 'readin' 'n writin' 'n 'rithmetic are possessed by all!

And today, her prayer is the prayer of a little boy who lived many years ago:

God help mother, help father, help sister,
Help everybody. TEACH ME TO READ AND
    WRITE.
Watch over Honey and make him a good dog;
And keep us all from getting lost in the wilderness.
    Amen!

That little boy lived and died before the days of Moonlight Schools—and he would have so appreciated them! His name was—Abraham Lincoln.

As I went walking down the way I met a pretty miss,
Who boldly looked at me and said: "A lovely day is this!"
Her hair was of a golden brown, her eyes a sparkling blue.
I proudly doffed my hat to her and answered, "Howdy-
    do!"

She placed her graceful hand in mine and turned to go
  my way,
Said I: "I have no time to flirt; I've work to do today,
I think you'd better run back home." With sadness
  dropped her chin.
"We'll pass the drug store soon," said she. "I thought
  you'd take me in."

"Oh, no," said I, "that wouldn't do. The hour is growing
  late
And I am on my way to town to keep a business date.
Besides, to make it very plain, no time for girls have I!"
At such a cold rebuff from me the maid began to cry.

Now, though I've been a married man for six-and-twenty
  years,
I haven't learned in all that time to cope with woman's
  tears.
And so I let that temptress fair, who's scarcely seven
  years old,
Escort me to the pharmacy where ice cream cones are sold.
                                      —*The Temptress*

CHRISTMAS SEALS

CHRISTMAS and tuberculosis don't mix. That's what the sceptics said. But to Emily Bissell, founder of the Anti-Tuberculosis Christmas Seals in America, these words were a challenge, a challenge to drive from the face of the earth the scourge, tuberculosis.

It was her untiring effort, her courage and perseverance that made possible the success of the Seals which in turn support the great and winning battle against the dread disease, tuberculosis. In 1907 Jacob A. Riis had written in the *Outlook Magazine* of Denmark's great success with the Christmas stamp. Mr. Riis, himself an immigrant, was greatly moved by the work accomplished by Einar Holboll, Danish "father of the Christmas stamp."

"Nothing in all the world is better proven today," wrote Riis, "than that tuberculosis is a preventable disease and therefore needless. Yet it goes on year after year killing an army of 150,000 persons and desolating countless homes in which half a million men and women are always wearily dragging themselves to graves dug by this single enemy. Perhaps I feel strongly about it, and no wonder. It killed six of my brothers, and I guess I know. That was in the days when there was no help for it. There is now."

Thus was planted the seed from which was to spring the fine work against the spread of tuberculosis. However, Fate was to place this work in the hands of a woman, a determined, far-seeing woman who was to accomplish a great humanitarian deed through hours of struggle, days of hard work. That woman was Emily P. Bissell. She was on the editorial staff of the *Outlook,* and read Jacob Riis's appeal with deep interest.

In 1907 she was Secretary of the Delaware Branch of the American Red Cross. Her cousin, Dr. Wales, was one of four doctors who had started a small sanitarium, one shack, in the woods near Brandy Wine Creek. Their money had run out, and they were afraid they would have to close the sanitarium. Dr. Wales appealed to Emily Bissell to help him raise $300 to continue the work.

Then it was that she resorted to the stamp that had been successful in Denmark. Fifty thousand were printed for forty dollars and were put on sale at a penny apiece. "It could only have been done at the time in a small community such as ours," says Miss Bissell.

The start was successful, but the enthusiasm of the first days soon dimmed, and Miss Bissell decided: "The Philadelphia 'North American' is popular here in Wilmington. Nearly everyone reads that paper. I'm going there and see if I can't enlist their aid."

But the Sunday editor of the newspaper told her, "I think you have a great cause, Miss Bissell, but I'm afraid you're on the wrong track. Tuberculosis and Merry Christmas don't mix. People don't want to be reminded of unpleasant things during the Christmas season."

Not to be turned aside, she appealed to Columnist Hodges, who was struck with the idea and promptly carried it to the managing editor. "Excuse me, Mr. Van Valkenburg," he said excitedly, "but you've gotta give me a minute. Look at these stamps. They're Christmas stamps. A Red Cross nurse named Bissell is trying to sell them in Wilmington. I tell you, Mr. Van Valkenburg, here's a way to wipe out tuberculosis!"

"I believe you're right, Hodges," agreed Van Valkenburg. "Yes, I'm convinced you are. Tell Miss Bissell the North American is hers for the holidays. Give her all the time you can spare and take all the space you need. Go to it. Tell every one of our readers about the Christmas stamps. Good luck!"

"And with confidence," wrote Hodges in his popular column, "we call upon every man, woman and child whose heart pulses with the warmth of humanity to join our ranks in driving this curse from the land; to buy these stamps according to the measure of each one's means and to mail no letter and send no package not decorated with these best of Christmas symbols of good will toward men."

The message of the Christmas stamp had been given to a nation which was ready to receive it. The national income from the sale of Christmas Seals each year now is a little over five million dollars. Eighty-five million dollars have been raised in the last thirty years by the seal. And tuberculosis in the last thirty years has been reduced in number of deaths from almost two hundred people per 100,000 population to about fifty-five. Tuberculosis is now the seventh disease in mortality.

[135]

The cheery, bright little stamps blazed their way across the nation, carrying their message of cheer and building up a strong reserve to combat the dread tuberculosis. Today, the ravages of this disease are held in check by skilled medical hands, but the chain that has been forged to accomplish this task is made up of tiny links, small bits of paper. Christmas Seals, carrying their message of mercy, and saying to all who see them: "Peace on Earth; Good Will to Men!"

There is many a battle that's yet to be won,
There is many a glorious deed to be done.
The world is still young! For the youth at its door
There are tasks some shall do never dreamed of before.
It is not an old world, worn and wrinkled and gray,
It's a world that is being reborn every day.

The old hearts are settled and fixed and they'll do
Nothing that's daring or brilliant or new.
Their days of adventure have long since gone by,
They have finished their tasks and they're waiting to die;
But the youngsters who stand at the world's open door
Have much to achieve never dreamed of before.

On the well-traveled lanes of the land and the sea
Every day will the crowds of humanity be.
On the streets which are paved and the avenue known
Are the people who care not to venture alone.

But the young heart and stout sees the goal that's afar,
And dares to set out where the strange dangers are.

What's not possible now shall be possible when
Some young heart and brave shows the way to all men.
Youth shall remake the world. What is best of today
Shall tomorrow to something that's better give way.
So, come you young fellows to life, with a will,
While you work and you dream the world cannot stand
    still.

                        —*Youth and the World*

TEN-FINGERED MICE

When a cake is nicely frosted and it's put away for tea,
And it looks as trim and proper as a chocolate cake
    should be,
Would it puzzle you at evening as you brought it from
    the ledge
To find the chocolate missing from its smooth and shiny
    edge?

As you viewed the cake in sorrow would you look around
    and say,
"Who's been nibbling in the pantry when he should have
    been at play?"
And if little eyes look guilty as they hungered for a slice,

Would you take Dad's explanation that it must have
   been the mice?

Oh, I'm sorry for the household that can keep a frosted
   cake
Smooth and perfect through the daytime, for the hearts
   of them must ache—
For it must be very lonely to be living in a house
Where the pantry's never ravaged by a glad ten-fingered
   mouse.

Though I've traveled far past forty, I confess that I,
   myself,
Even now will nip a morsel from the good things on
   the shelf;
And I never blame the youngsters who discover chocolate
   cake
For the tiny little samples which exultantly they take.

RICHES TO RAGS, AND BACK TO RICHES

FROM riches to rags, and from rags back to riches again; that is the story of Mrs. Alice Foote MacDougall, mother, business executive, famous restaurant owner—a courageous woman who today at seventy is an outstanding example of "It Can Be Done."

Alice Foote MacDougall was born to riches and schooled as a child of wealth. She was the granddaughter of one of New York's first families. Her grandfather, the Honorable Stephen Allen, Mayor of New York City, occupied an important position both socially and politically.

Born in 1867, Alice was brought up by governesses among the elite. Surrounded by luxury, trained to be a "lady," she was indeed ill-equipped for the years that were to follow. She was married to the handsome Allan MacDougall. They had everything—youth, good looks, money, social position.

Soon came motherhood: three lovely children, Gladys, Allan and Don. And then, just when she should have had the security she might have expected, the fates conspired against her husband. His coffee business went under. "We haven't a thing left, absolutely nothing," he glumly told her.

"Listen to me, Allan," she replied. "We have a lot left. We have each other and we have our children. Why, you're not going to let this misfortune stop you. We'll sell your own coffee formula."

But just as they were about to make the new start, about to rebuild their fortune, Allan MacDougall died. Alice now faced the future alone with her three children, and without funds.

Evicted from her premises by the sheriff, Mrs. Mac-Dougall quietly decided that her real struggle with life had just begun. She was forty, a widow, and had thirty-eight dollars. Faced with all possible odds, her life be-clouded with grim disappointment, her outlook obscured by despair, this courageous woman faced the future with typical American determination to prove to a doubting world that a woman could embark on a business career and become an outstanding success.

In the office of her friend, J. Noah Slee, she discussed with him the not too bright future. "And so," said he, "Mrs. MacDougall, you've rented the little office at 129 Front Street?"

"Yes, Mr. Slee," she replied, "I took a year's lease. The rental for twelve months will be $250. I didn't have the money for furniture, so I'm using a packing box. But I did buy a bin for blending my coffee. Do you think I can make a go of it? All the men in the district are laughing at me."

"Mrs. MacDougall," said Slee, "you might as well get used to one thing. Make up your mind that throughout life, no matter what you try to do, you'll meet with dis-couragement on every side. I say to you, make up your mind that you're going to make a success of your busi-ness; forget what the doubting Thomasses are saying, and then go ahead and do it. *I* believe in you, and I'll guarantee you to the amount of $500. Good luck!"

Alice Foote MacDougall bravely carried on in the face of odds, against the predictions of her competitors she fought out the battle alone. Because she had practically no capital, she did everything herself, canvassing, selling, making up orders and delivering them to her customers. Nothing was too burdensome for this determined pioneer business woman.

One day she thought of the thousands and thousands of people who go through Grand Central Terminal every day on their way to trains. "A coffee shop in the Grand Central Terminal," she thought, "might do very well. We'll give people *good* coffee, the *best* coffee in New York."

That was Alice Foote MacDougall's motto then, and it is her motto now. The coffee shop was a success. Soon she opened six other eating places, each patterned after a quiet, restful European cafe. Mrs. MacDougall was a success as a restaurateur. New York liked her restaurants. Diners flocked to them. Soon her business was grossing $1,684,000 a year!

Then came the depression. In 1932, Mrs. MacDougall, like countless others, lost her business. Her six restaurants went into receivership, but Alice Foote MacDougall at sixty-five years of age, was not ready to admit defeat. At sixty-five, she started on the comeback trail, believing that America has always come back and that she would come back with it.

Today, at seventy, she has arrived again. She is pro-
prietress of three flourishing restaurants, feeding between
three thousand and five thousand persons a day. She even
now "lays out the coffee" for the men to pack and ship.
It's her own blend, and she believes "nothing in the world
can even touch it."

At seventy years of age still actively engaged in life's
vineyard, she retains the spirit that has drawn America
ever forward.

In the days of long ago every lady had to know
    How to paint a bunch of pansies on each saucer, cup
      and plate,
And a butter dish where grew no pink rosebud wouldn't
    do,
    Since the fashion called for china most peculiarly ornate.

I wonder if at all those lost splendors you recall
    When the stuff they called "hand-painted" was the very
      smartest thing;
When the plainest gravy boat had carnations at its throat,
    And every dish of spinach wore the violets of spring.

Plates and cups were edged with gold, just as thick as
    they could hold,
    And we stared at purple pansies as we bent to cool our
      soup;
Then the crocus used to flash through the steaming corned
    beef hash,

And beneath the mashed potatoes bloomed a lovely
floral group.

But today nobody spills salt from fields of daffodils,
And the ham and eggs no longer rest on beds of as-
phodel.
Where the greasy pork chops lie, not one blossom greets
the eye.
Those "hand-painted" days have vanished, and I think
it's just as well.

—Hand-Painted China Days

THE FAMILY DOCTOR

I've tried the high-toned specialists, who doctor folks
to-day;
I've heard the throat man whisper low "Come on now
let us spray;"
I've sat in fancy offices and waited long my turn,
And paid for fifteen minutes what it took a week to earn;
But while these scientific men are kindly, one and all,
I miss the good old doctor that my mother used to call.

The old-time family doctor! Oh, I am sorry that he's
gone,
He ushered us into the world and knew us every one;
He didn't have to ask a lot of questions, for he knew
Our histories from birth and all the ailments we'd been
through.

[143]

And though as children small we feared the medicines
 he'd send,
The old-time family doctor grew to be our dearest
 friend.

No hour too late, no night too rough for him to heed our
 call;
He knew exactly where to hang his coat up in the hall;
He knew exactly where to go, which room upstairs to
 find
The patient he'd been called to see, and saying: "Never
 mind,
I'll run up there myself and see what's causing all the
 fuss."
It seems we grew to look and lean on him as one of us.

He had a big and kindly heart, a fine and tender way,
And more than once I've wished that I could call him
 in to-day.
The specialists are clever men and busy men, I know,
And haven't time to doctor as they did long years ago;
But some day he may come again, the friend that we can
 call,
The good old family doctor who will love us one and all.

SOFT SOAP

Lester Gaba, sculptor and designer extraordinary, might well be called "the man who carved a career in soap;" for Lester Gaba, yesterday a boy in Hannibal, Missouri, is today at the top of his profession through skillful handling of a cake of soap. Today, the soap figurines and wax models of this youngster of thirty-one are known throughout the world. But behind the success story of Lester Gaba, there is another story—a tale of a typical American boy who was bound and determined to succeed.

At ten, Lester, had already shown a marked aptitude for the art which was to distinguish him. In the Gaba home at Hannibal one day a group of his playmates entered through the kitchen door. "H'yah, fellas, come on in," Lester greeted them.

"*You* c'mon out," replied one of the boys. "What's the idea, stayin' inside a swell day like this? We're goin' fishin'. Get your . . ."

"Can't," answered Lester. "Gotta finish."

"Finish what?"

"This soap carving. A lady sent me a clipping about it. See? If I win, I get a dandy prize."

"If you win? Watcha trying to cut outa that hunk of soap?"

"It's a juggler," explained Lester. "That is, it's gonna

be a juggler, and he's gonna be just like he was throwin' the balls."

"Ha. That's a good one. What's gonna keep the balls up in the air?"

Lester Gaba didn't quite figure out how to finish the juggler for the soap contest, and as the days went on, like the other boys, he *did* go fishing and forgot about sculpture in soap. Then, at the age of fifteen, he left high school at Hannibal to go to Chicago. There he secured work as a delivery boy and studied drawing at night at the Academy of Fine Arts.

He failed to make a hit doing some work for the head of the advertising department of some movie theatres, but a lobby display of some of his soap figures at the stage presentation of "The Wax Museum" attracted some favorable attention. But the future looked none too bright and in 1928 when Lester was twenty-one, his father died and he returned to Hannibal. It looked at the time as though he had come to a definite turn in the artistic road which was yet to bring him fame and fortune.

At this point of his life, he began toying with the craft in which he was to win his reputation. One day he fashioned a miniature of Napoleon. "I'll be jiggered," commented a friend on seeing the model. "That's perfect."

"Like it?" asked Lester.

"I think it's swell. You know, you ought to do something with that. I'll bet you somebody would pay for things like that."

"I wish I could find that somebody," replied Lester. Then he snapped his fingers and added, "You know, that gives me an idea. I think I'll go to New York. I have a hunch that, if I'm ever going to get anywhere, I'll have to go out and *find my discoverer!* Something tells me they're not going to find *me!*"

So twenty-two-year-old Lester Gaba headed for New York, armed with courage, confidence and a few drawings and bits of soap sculpture. On an impulse he went to see Neysa McMein, the famous illustrator.

"I'm afraid, Mr. Gaba," she told him, "that you have a great deal more to do, that you must put a great deal more study on your drawings."

"Oh, I understand," he replied.

"But these little soap sculptures are marvelous! They're grand. And I'll tell you what I'm going to do. I'm going to a friend of mine who's head of the art department of a big advertising agency. I'm going to ask him to look over your work."

In that way he got a chance to do a soap figure for an advertisement. His work was something new, and soon there was a demand for it. But along came the depression, and, like so many other things, the soap figures of Lester Gaba were forgotten. For a year he lived with relatives on a farm in New York state, doing odd jobs for his board and room.

Then one day he decided to return to New York. Finally, after walking forty blocks to see the editor, he sold a sketch to a magazine for fifty dollars. That sale was a turning point. From then on the years of grit and determination began to pay dividends. Soon, his soap sculptures became known throughout the world. But the creative genius of Lester Gaba was not yet through. He turned to the design of wax figures of women for window displays, and soon the Gaba Girls were as famous as the glamorous Gibson girls of another day.

Then came "Cynthia," the most glamorous of them all, a full-sized doll, who accompanies him to theatres, night clubs and other public places—as Gaba explains, "a plaster composition image of feminine pulchritude." This mannequin companion is now nationally famous.

Lester Gaba's models are as well-known in New York's smart windows, as Lester himself is among New York's smart set. Among the prominent figures he has designed in soap are Popeye, Shirley Temple, many of Frank Buck's animals, Orphan Annie and Charlie McCarthy. In addition he is very active a great part of the time in designing packages, costume jewelry, fabrics and magazine illustrations.

Gaba agrees that one of the things that gave him a start in New York was the "Soapy Circus." "It was made up," he recalls, "of a zebra, an elephant and a lion, all made in soap, and they were safely contained in a little painted wagon that children could pull. Incidentally, these were the first American designed soap figures. There had been soap figures before, but all had been imported from Czechoslovakia."

"Somehow or other," Gaba says, "I have had a feeling

that I have wanted to keep my work alive with a very definite American touch. That is one reason I have avoided European trips in the past. My background and my inspiration are entirely American. Any success I may have achieved I owe to my American background."

Thus once again is proved, in this story of the small-town boy who made good in the big city, that determination, stick-to-itiveness and talent cannot be denied! Lester Gaba, his story, is a brilliant case in point for every young American: a case in point that here in America there is equal opportunity for everyone.

Suppose, for a minute, you stumbled and fell
To the bottom, we'll say, of a ninety-foot well,
And nobody heard you or answered your shout,
Would you lie there and die, and not try to get out?

Suppose you were cornered, we'll say, by a brute,
With no one to throw you a rifle to shoot,
With no one to help in your terrible plight,
Would you give up your life without making a fight?

Well, this little trouble which has you upset
Is nothing compared to what others have met;
So why do you whimper and whine o'er your case,
Why give up and quit without making the race?

Remember, my boy, when you're troubled by doubt,
From caverns of gloom men have worked their way out.

[149]

When the Fates have you cornered, your courage must
    show—
Don't lie down and die at the very first blow.

—Against Odds

TWO SOURCES OF WEALTH

Wealth comes out of the earth, they say—
    The golden grain and the metals cold.
Out of the ground comes the toiler's pay.
    Out of the ground comes the rich man's gold.

Then whence come laughter and lilting song,
    And whence come friendships for men to find?
Whence comes choice between right and wrong?
    Out of the heart and out of the mind.

Two real sources of wealth has man;
    But over the earth may the tempest sweep
And the riches gathered by pick and pan
    Are easier found than they are to keep.

But that other wealth of the heart and mind
    Which is coined in wisdom and mirth and song
And makes man friendly and makes him kind
    Enriches him for his whole life long.

LADY SCOUT

MRS. ROY LARGENT, a charming woman from McKinney, Texas, holds a position unique in the annals of the sports world. She is a "baseball scout" who digs up in the sticks the young player-talent that keeps the big leagues flourishing.

Several years ago Mrs. Largent was sitting in the stands at the practice field of the McKinney High School baseball field watching her husband put his players through their paces. In the empty stands behind the catcher she sat there placidly knitting.

Presently a man came in and sat down beside her. "I was just driving by," he remarked. "You see, I'm kind of a nut on baseball."

"A real fan, eh?" she replied.

"Yeah, I'm a fan all right. Never miss a game any city I hit. Guess I'll never get over wanting to be a big league player. Always imagined I'd be a great shortstop when I was a kid. Say, you must be quite a fan yourself, sitting out here for practice."

"Well, you see, I . . . "

"Don't blame you. It's a great game. Kind a slick. Watch the boys play and knit at the same time."

"Yes," she explained, "I enjoy trying to pick out the most likely boys early in the season and . . . "

"An amateur scout, eh?"

"Sort of. I study all the boys who try out for the team

[151]

every season. And then I try to make up my mind as to which one would be the best pitcher, catcher and so forth. It's really . . . "

"Sort of a hobby, eh, Mrs. . . . "

"Largent."

"Matter of fact, I'll bet you'd do a better job than that coach out there. Why, he . . . "

"That coach does pretty well," retorted Mrs. Largent. "You see, he's a scout for the Chicago White Sox!"

Thus Mrs. Largent began her career by watching her husband, noted White Sox scout, coach the McKinney High School nine. From her seat in the bleachers she developed an eye for talent, a thorough-going knowledge of what it takes to make a real baseball player.

Then one evening she received a letter from Mr. Lou Comiskey, President of the White Sox, saying that he had heard a lot about her and asking if she would like to be a scout for them. And that's how Mrs. Roy Largent became America's only woman baseball scout, a position hitherto sacredly reserved for men.

During the fourteen years following her appointment, Mrs. Largent has traveled over 400,000 miles looking for promising young ball players. And she has found her portion of them, too.

She discovered Luke Appling, 1936 American League batting champion; Big Zeke Bonura, first-baseman now with Washington and Pitcher Johnny Whitehead, to say nothing of Vernon Kennedy, Monty Stratton and Rip Radcliff.

Yes, Mrs. Roy Largent proved that it can be done and had time to tend to her knitting at the same time!

There is in life this golden chance
    For every valiant soul,
The unpenned poem or romance—
    The undiscovered goal.

Beyond the sum of all we know
    And all that man has done,
Life holds a never-ending row
    Of glories to be won.

Still waits the canvas for the paint,
    The paper for the pen;
Still searches Faith to find a saint
    Among the ranks of men.

Though man, it seems, has traveled far
    Along achievement's way,
His conquests and his triumphs are
    But splendors for a day.

In all that is of paint and print,
    And marvels which we see,
Life gives us but the faintest hint
    Of splendors yet to be.

On still untraveled roads of fame
    The feet of men shall climb

Far nobler goals than ours to claim
From the rich lap of time.

Unreckoned genius yet unborn
Undreamed of deeds shall do.
Night ends the old. With every morn
Life bids us start the new.

—The Golden Chance

THE QUITTER

Because he sulked and hung his head
When turned the battle bitter,
The spirit from his body fled.
It couldn't stand a quitter.

GRIDIRON WIZARD

THIS is the story of a little fellow who wouldn't quit, wouldn't quit against all odds until he had won—the story of Robert C. Zuppke, head football coach at the University of Illinois since 1913, and maker of seven Big Ten championship and two National championship gridiron elevens. Sports writers acclaim him as one of the nation's greatest coaches. Under Bob Zuppke have studied some of football's foremost players and coaches. Everywhere when gridiron enthusiasts meet, the name of Zuppke holds a magic significance.

Back in 1901 Bob Zuppke was an undergraduate at the University of Wisconsin, slight, wiry, under-weight, but doggedly determined to make the husky Badger football team. But the best he could do, because of his small build, was to stay on the scrubs and scrimmage the varsity, make cannon fodder for the regulars.

Game, as determined as a toy bulldog, the midget mixed with the Wisconsin varsity giants and earned their unqualified admiration. Injuries did not deter him, nor the hopeless prospect of getting into a game. Saturday afternoon upon Saturday afternoon as the Cardinal and Gray engaged their opponents on the gridiron, on the substitute bench, along with the other scrubs sat Bob Zuppke, cheering and studying.

This was the undergraduate football career of Robert C. Zuppke, the inglorious career of a weekday worker who

[155]

got the bruises and who sat on the substitute bench during game-time when glory was to be had. Night after night during the football season, a weary, battered little figure would hurry from the practice field, eat a cold supper and trudge to his study room. One such evening, his roommate, Jim, jumped on him. "I've got something to say, Zup. Something you may not like?"

"What's on your mind, Jim?" snapped Zup. "Spill it."

"Well, it's like this, Zup. I . . . I hate to say it, but for two years I've been watching you come home from football practice, bruised, stiff, more dead than alive."

"Well?"

"Well, what do you expect it's gonna get you? You know you're too small to make the team."

"Maybe."

"Maybe, my eye," grumbled Jim. "There's no sense in your trying; it can't be done. Besides, this business of football and trying to be an artist just don't mix. Now, if you'd just be sensible and give up getting shellacked at practice every night and just stay with your painting."

"I don't know that I want to be an artist, Jim," said Zuppke.

"I get it," replied Jim sarcastically. "You want to be an All-American and paint pictures on the side. Keep on the way you're going and you won't be anything."

"Maybe and maybe not," replied the resolute Zuppke. "You see, Jim, I may be too small to *play* football, but that doesn't mean I can't learn *how* to play it."

And Bob Zuppke did learn *how* to play football. His tiny figure, huddled on the substitutes' bench, burned with intensity as he studied every play. In the class room, he was equally intent, majoring in psychology, the better to understand his great love, football. Hoping against hope that he would be called upon to play for his alma mater, Bob Zuppke "sat out" his football career.

Then came the day of his graduation and an offer to teach history and coach football at the Madison, Wisconsin High School. But Zuppke decided not to take it. "I'm going to New York," he said, "to see if I really know anything about art."

With thirty-four dollars, he went to the metropolis and with the same dogged determination that had made him haunt the gridiron, he haunted New York's art centers. His father had been a jewelry designer for Tiffany's, and Zuppke had the artist's touch. For a spell he painted on a big cigar sign high above Broadway. But all the while he was torn between two desires—his love of art, and his love of football.

The pigskin pastime soon won out, however, and after a year, Zuppke became football coach at Muskegon, Michigan. A victorious season and an undisputed state title brought him to Oak Park High School at Oak Park, Illinois. There, his team lost its first engagement and never lost a game under his tutelage from that time on, capturing a national championship.

Then the sporting world was surprised when this successful "high school" coach was signed as coach at the

University of Illinois for the season of 1913. There was much skepticism among the know-alls.

The first evening Zuppke went out on old "Illinois field" north of the old Gym was on Friday the thirteenth in 1913, and the first thing he saw on the ground was a lemon. "What chance is there for me," he wrote his brother in Minneapolis that night. "I start work on Friday the thirteenth, 1913, and the first thing I see is a lemon."

"Your job," wrote back his brother, "is to take that lemon off that field."

And Zuppke did it!

In 1914, his second year on the job, with Harold Pogue, "Potsy" Clark, Bart Macomber, "Slooey" Chapman and that great crew, Illinois won the Big Ten championship. Zuppke still says that team was his best, because it had the most speed. But his other Illinois championship teams of 1915, 1918, 1919, 1923, 1927 and 1928 also all had their points.

And as Zuppke points out: "Many good teams never win championships. Our 1933 team lost a tie for first place by two points, missed goals after touchdowns, and the 1934 team lost a tie for first also by losing one game by a margin of four points. There we lost two championships by six points. That's football for you."

Zuppke rates Red Grange his greatest student. "I believe he was the greatest, bar none," he says, "who played anywhere, any time. His name will live longer in the legends of football than any other. He did more things.

They say you can't have everything, but Grange as a player did have everything."

"Football," Zuppke says, "is more than a game—it is a spirit. Boys like to play it because it appeals to their imagination, to the same spirit of adventure which sent the pioneers into the unknown, sent Lindbergh over the Atlantic and Byrd over the poles. It is the hero urge.

"Football teaches a boy to stand on his own feet. The player competes directly against another. He finds that the only way he can take the job away from the other fellow is by merit. Money, position, influence, politics—all count for nothing. If football didn't have so many positive virtues it would have been destroyed long ago by the envious enemies created by its success."

And Zuppke believes that football helps many a boy to win a personal success. Their school-day contacts with this little man who fought his way to the top undoubtedly is invaluable to them. "I tell them," Zuppke says, *"to keep moving*. That goes for athletics, for business and the professions. One of our old football players who has been exceptionally successful exemplifies this maxim. They said of him that when his associates sat around and talked about *what* to do, he took a train and did it. I also say: 'Don't let hope elude you.' If you do, it will prove the costliest fumble of your life. The greatest failure to me is the boy with ability who only half tries. I will say that the stern discipline of football often corrects this."

As for his painting, which lately has been winning more and more praise from the critics, Zuppke says, "I paint only for the pure love of it and do not pretend to be a professional. I never paint, or golf either, during the football season, but in other periods it's a fine avocation. Anyway, athletics and painting have much in common. They both demand the 'touch' that is so necessary in athletics, and the ability to concentrate and the physical endurance to paint powerfully over every inch of canvas. If you could tie a brush to a football player in motion you would get a beautifully graceful, rhythmic design. But no painting can match the picture presented when eleven fine young physical specimens, full of symmetry and rhythm, run out on a green gridiron on a golden October day."

Bob Zuppke was too small to "make the team." Too small to earn a "letter" on the varsity. But he wasn't too small to show a doubting world that "it could be done." His courage, his shrewdness, his insight, his coaching ability and influence over his players brought Illinois to the top. It was he who invented the famous razzle-dazzle style of play and the "huddle." It is said he has more gridiron creations to his credit than any other coach. The screen-pass and on-side kick plays devised by him were stopped only by legislation in the rules. Yes, and it is the same Robert Zuppke whose paintings are admired by critics and laymen at his yearly exhibits in New York and Chicago. You see, Bob Zuppke's the kind of little fellow, who just won't quit!

I'd rather fancied it would come, a healthy boy who's ten
    years old
Forecasts the things he'll want to do without his secrets
    being told;
And so last night when I got home and found his mother
    strangely still,
I guessed somehow that mother love had battled with a
    youngster's will.
"You'll have to settle it," said she; "there's nothing more
    that I can say,
The game of football's calling him and he insists he
    wants to play."

We've talked it over many a time; we've hoped he
    wouldn't choose the game,
And I suppose there's not a boy whose parents do not
    feel the same.
They dread, as we, the rugged sport; they wonder, too,
    just what they'll say
When son of theirs comes home, as ours, and begs to be
    allowed to play.
And now the question's up to me, a question that I can't
    evade,
But football is a manly game and I am glad he's not afraid.

He wants to play, he says to me; he knows the game is
    rough and grim,
But worse than hurt and broken bones is what his friends
    will think of him;

"They'd call me yellow," he explained, "if I stay out."
    Of all things here
There's nothing quite so hard to bear as is the heartless
    gibe or jeer,
And though I cannot spare him pain or hurt when tackles
    knock him flat,
Being his father, I've said "yes," because I choose to
    spare him that.

                      —*Football*

HONOR

Honor, with everything at stake,
Fine choice of methods still will make
And chooses, rather than to cheat
To suffer nothing but defeat.

CORN BELT TRADER HORN

WANT to "swap"? Feel like "tradin' "? Looking for a fair "exchange"? Then see John S. Redshaw, the "Modern Trader Horn" at Granville, Illinois. For in this quiet little town near Peoria, Illinois, lives the man who has modernized the ancient art of trading.

Here, in the midst of his vast treasure houses of gems, antiques and rare objects of art, sits the American version of the ancient Oriental barterer! John S. Redshaw is a trader, a merchant who buys and sells anything, and his rise from obscurity to international repute is truly a saga of the crowded pages of bustling American business life.

One of a family of six children, Mr. Redshaw was born in Spring Valley, Illinois, the son of a coal miner. One of his early pleasures was studying a mail order catalogue "window fishing." He got almost as much fun out of looking at all those things as if he really had them. He was the kind of boy with a big bump of curiosity. He read, he noticed, he looked at everything. And soon he began swapping, in a small way, among his friends: a hoop and stick and two cigar coupons for a jack-knife; the jack-knife, plus four real aggies and a stickpin for a watch-chain. Then he wondered how he could get a *watch* with it!

Thus John S. Redshaw prepared himself for the career he was to carve out. Swapping, trading, studying relative values, the boy grew older. When the war came, he went

over. John came back, and became postmaster at Granville.

He began trading fountain pens, bamboo fountain pens
that would write, to men whose fountain pens wouldn't
write. He ran ads in the papers, and began swapping
his gun collection. Next, he had rented the bank building
to run a swap-shop! There wasn't a single price tag in
the place. He remembered everything in his head.

For Mr. Redshaw is more than a trader of worldly
goods; he's a trader of articles that have no price. A
party wished to purchase a diamond. In return he offered
a horse and a wheelchair. The deal was consummated,
and the party went home satisfied. In another instance,
Redshaw had in stock a very beautiful genuine ruby surrounded by fifty diamonds, set in a beautiful platinum
ring. A party wanted this ring and offered in exchange
an entire carload of assorted hardware, consisting of
everything from general hardware to automobile acces-
sories. Again he traded a cow for a piano, a fur coat for
an expensive dog, a pair of live raccoons for a thousand
cans of paint, a radio set for pork sausages, silverware
for a totem pole, binoculars for a baby carriage and an
outboard motor for a lot of petticoats!

"We have," says Mr. Redshaw, "an exceptionally fine
Mandarin Robe into whose gold-brocade went more than
seven years of hand-work. I also have a Japanese ivory
sheathed hara-kiri knife—an exceptionally rare treasure,
its value being enhanced because the blood of its victim
still remains on its razor-sharp blade. We have a fur

robe, quilted, containing approximately two thousand pieces of every known fur. The robe was traded to me by a widow whose husband had hunted every fur-bearing animal known around the world. You see, a man's worth can never be determined by what he has in cash. Many things have real value in life besides money. As we walk down life's pathway, sentimental values take on an added importance. We have in our possession, for instance, one of the few miniature carvings made by the late Anton Lang, the celebrated impersonator of Christ, from Oberammergau, Germany, and it is one of the pieces in our vast collection that causes almost everyone to stop and have a second look.

"At times we have had as many as twenty saddle horses; five hundred canaries. And by the way they all got loose at one time in the office, flew in every which direction, and it was only with the aid of flashlights in the night that we were able to retrieve them.

"I have had sixty dogs, and two hundred and sixty rabbits on hand at one time, along with collections of art, musical instruments, lathes and all kinds of machinery, bowling alleys, store fixtures. And add to all these, one collection of seven thousand bird eggs.

"But it's fun. There is something different every day. Occasionally the picture changes. Now and then perhaps trouble strikes—the family farm has been foreclosed, an injunction has been served on the bank balance, taking all their worldly wealth, all save those precious treasured heirlooms handed down from generation to generation.

"It is then that our business becomes at once both difficult and pleasant. Pleasant because we can find a way
to dispose of those things and give them the cash they
need, and difficult because it is always hard to see anyone
in trouble. This is our opportunity to serve."

Trading, an American heritage long dead, has been revived by John Redshaw. Large or small, he will swap
anything. For the spirit of the ancient barterer is in the
bloodstream of this man from Granville, "the gentleman
of swap."

It isn't the money you're making, it isn't the clothes you
    wear,
And it isn't the skill of your good right hand which makes
    folks really care.
It's the smile on your face and the light of your eye and
    the burdens that you bear.

Most any old man can tell you, most any old man at all,
Who has lived through all sorts of weather, winter and
    summer and fall,
That riches and fame are shadows that dance on the
    garden wall.

It's how do you live and neighbor, how do you work and
    play,
It's how do you say "good morning" to the people along
    the way,

And it's how do you face your troubles whenever your
    skies are gray.

It's you, from the dawn to the night time; you when the
    day is fair,
You when the storm is raging—how do you face despair?
It is you that the world discovers, whatever the clothes
    you wear.

You to the end of the journey, kindly and brave and true,
The best and the worst of you gleaming in all that you
    say and do,
And the thing that counts isn't money, or glory or power,
    but you!

—What Counts

GOD MADE THIS DAY FOR ME

Jes' the sort o' weather and jes' the sort o' sky
Which seem to suit my fancy, with the white clouds
    driftin' by
On a sea o' smooth blue water. Oh, I ain't an egotist,
With an "I" in all my thinkin', but I'm willin' to insist
That the Lord that made us humans an' the birds in
    every tree
Knows my special sort o' weather an' He made this day
    fer me.

This is jes' my style o' weather—sunshine floodin' all the
    place,

[167]

An' the breezes from the eastward blowin' gently on my
    face.
An' the woods chock-full o' singin' till you'd think birds
    never had
A single care to fret 'em or a grief to make 'em sad.
Oh, I settle down contented in the shadow of a tree,
An' tell myself right proudly that the day was made fer
    me.

It's my day, sky an' sunshine, an' the temper o' the breeze.
Here's the weather I would fashion could I run things as
    I please—
Beauty dancin' all around me, music ringin' everywhere,
Like a weddin' celebration. Why, I've plumb fergot my
    care
An' the tasks I should be doin' fer the rainy days to be,
While I'm huggin' the delusion that God made this day
    fer me.

THE MOUNTY

COUNTLESS miles of barren waste, land ice-covered since the beginning of time, across whose surface falls the shimmering light of the aurora borealis. Land of the midnight sun, land of frozen rivers, impassable rivers, impregnable forests. Such is the country of the Canadian far north, such the rim of the arctic where bad men seek shelter, where countless crimes have been committed, where murder once ran rampant.

To whom does Canada look for law and order in these barren waste lands? To whom does she turn for the policing on this frontier? It is the Royal Canadian Mounted Police who so ably govern this territory. You have seen them, perhaps, those stalwart men whose immaculate scarlet jackets, whose broad brimmed Stetsons, breeches and boots mark them as men apart.

It is to these fearless, hard-riding, red-coated stalwarts that Canada owes its thanks for the law-abiding rule of their frozen frontier. Every day of Sergeant Sidney Clay's twenty-two-year service on the rim of the Arctic has been filled with experiences that were a challenge to life itself. Daring, hardship and deprivation, are all contained in the words: "Serve our King," "Uphold the right."

Sidney Clay, a native of Somersetshire, England, joined the Royal Canadian Mounted Police at the age of twenty-three, after service as a trooper with the Imperial Yeomanry, Forty-eighth Squadron in the Boer War in South Africa.

After six months of intensive training and instruction, he received his first assignment into the then newly opened Yukon territory where the natives of that wild region quickly learned that the scarlet-coated Mounted Police were to be respected, that their word was the law of this wilderness. But there remained those who were yet to learn, those who had not yet crossed the path of the young, determined Sidney Clay. Making his way through the brush-covered trail leading to Edson, Clay came upon a sixteen pack horse train.

Promptly he challenged the three men, "Stop in the name of the Crown!"

"Well, what's the idea?"

"I'm a Royal Canadian Mounted," Clay explained. "Stand aside till I search your pack."

"There's nothing in these packs, keep your hands off," commanded one of the men, a Mexican. "This goods belongs to us."

"Stand back," ordered Clay. "I'm going to search these packs." And he proceeded to do it. In a moment, he said, "Well, whiskey, and a lot of it. You boys know this is prohibition territory and you know you can't bring this whiskey in. Come with . . . "

"Stop! We go our own way. Listen, like in Mexico, I will pump you full of lead."

"Give me that gun, and yours, too, partner. That's it. Now, pull your horses. We're going to make a little jaunt back to the justice of the peace. It's just eighty miles."

Convicted before the justice of the peace, the men were fined $200 each and their goods confiscated. "Good job you did, Clay," praised the justice of the peace, "in bringing that outfit to the bar. I congratulate you. Bringing in three men, sixteen horses and your own pack, well, that's what I call impossible."

Some time afterward, while out on the trail, a bullet pierced Clay's hat. "Look, Pretty Boy," said Clay to his horse. "A horse and his rider, our Mexican friend." The Mexican tried to out-run the Mounty, but Clay winged him. Again the Mounty got his man.

The next assignment given Sergeant Clay took him far into the Northwest, where with a party of thirty valiant men, he blazed a trail from the Yukon clear to British Columbia. His next trip took him east along the Arctic coast to the mouth of the Coppermine River, up the river to Bloody Falls, then to Great Bear Lake. Then two hundred miles across the lake and a hundred miles to the McKenzie River—600 miles in all!

At Fort Normand, they found that the dogs couldn't make it over the ice, and they decided to take recourse in a big scow when the ice broke up. When the ice went out, they set off on the 600 miles to Fort McPherson only to run into an ice jam which crushed the scow. For two hours Sidney Clay jumped from ice cake to ice cake. At last, cut, battered, bruised, wet and half frozen, he made the shore—alone! Later, however, he discovered that his companion, Corporal Cornelius, also had made it.

That's the spirit of the Royal Canadian Mounted Police. They were in desperate circumstances, but they didn't give up. They unraveled their clothes and made rabbit snares. They suffered, but they fought their way through to accomplish their mission.

Sidney Clay was soon back on duty. Then came an assignment that was to take him again into the Yukon, the brawling, boisterous Yukon of the Gold Rush Days, a Yukon that Robert Service knew.

Sergeant Clay entered by the "back door," unannounced.

"I'm here to ask about Michael LaRoque, wanted for murder," he stated. "You know where he is?"

"I, that is, maybe you'd better not look too hard for LaRoque, Sergeant," was the reply.

"I asked you if you knew where Michael LaRoque was."

"No. I don't. But I can tell you what he said."

"Go on."

"He said, 'Tell Clay to look out if he comes after me. My gun's as good as his!'"

With this warning did Sergeant Clay start after Michael LaRoque, murderer. With the typical calm of the Force on any assignment, whether it be to bring aid to an injured trapper, or to track down a desperate murderer, Sidney Clay set about his work, single-handed. He found LaRoque's trail and followed it.

As he advanced, Clay reasoned to himself: "So, I'll cut myself a length of pine. Your gun may be as good as mine, but somehow, I've found a stout club is usually a pretty good persuader!"

Then he stalked his game.

"I want you, LaRoque!"

"Why, you dirty . . . "

There followed the sound of a blow, a chair over-turning and the thud of fists.

"All right, Sergeant, all right," panted LaRoque. "You win. I'll go!"

LaRoque's words were typical of the respect commanded by the Royal Canadian Mounted Police, all through the northern wilds.

As Sergeant Clay explains, "A member of the Force stationed in the far north is, of course, primarily a police officer. However, he is also expected to act as a magistrate, a coroner, game guardian, registrar of vital statistics, postmaster, game warden, commissioner of wrecks, customs collector and any other small job that the government may desire to wish upon him."

Approximately 1200 men comprise this famous police body, men whose courage in the face of danger, whose perseverance in the fact of handicap are testimonials proving over and over again that "It Can Be Done."

I watched a candle burning at a banquet table spread,
Adding just a touch of beauty by the mellow light it shed,
But strangely in the center was the tallest of the lot,
Which was purposely unlighted or by chance had been
    forgot.

The burning candles glistened; every lovely beam they
threw
Brought them nearer to their death beds when they'd die
as candles do,
But the one they'd left unlighted stayed a golden taper
tall,
Still retaining all its freshness, giving out no light at all.

Then I wondered as I watched them, are we all like candles made,
With the gift of light within us, but to use it up afraid?
Do we hope that life may miss us and, forgetful, pass
us by
While our fellows burn in service for the joy they can
supply?

—Burning Candle

HOME-MADE CANDY

ONCE a woman took an egg and a cup of sugar—total cost five cents—and with these ingredients she made a batch of candy. She sold that candy, made another batch, and another, and another. Today, twenty-nine years later, she is active head of a group of America's outstanding candy stores and an American business leader in her own right. A simple formula for success, you say? Not quite. Not by many, many obstacles overcome and adversities hurdled by a courageous, gallant woman, Mrs. Ora H. Snyder.

Ora Hanson began making a home for her father and her older brothers and sisters when she herself was but a child of twelve. The motherless child grew into a fine young woman who was married at eighteen. In Maywood, Illinois, the Snyder home was a typical happy American home.

But to that happy family came misfortune, as Mr. Snyder, assistant paymaster for a large corporation, was stricken with typhoid fever. As the weeks passed and her husband grew steadily worse, Mrs. Snyder, the young housewife who had never been faced with a care or worry since her marriage, resolutely faced an uncertain future.

One day to a neighborhood school store she went and said to the proprietor, "Mrs. Lee, I . . . I wonder if you'd do something for me."

"Why certainly, dear," replied the kind lady. "I'd be glad to . . . "

"You see, I, well, I made a batch of my divinity fudge. I have it here, and I wondered if you'd sell it to the school children who come . . . "

"Why, Ora," replied Mrs. Lee. "It would be a blessing to be able to offer candy as good and wholesome as yours to the children. It'll be the biggest penny's worth those tots have got in a long time."

The youngsters *did* appreciate Ora Snyder's candy, and the little neighborhood candy store teemed with activity as chubby little fists extended pennies for Mrs. Snyder's wonderful dainties. But, not satisfied with having staved off the financial disaster which had threatened her home, as her husband regained his health she spoke to him about further inroads into the business world.

"I've been thinking," she told him, "of taking my candy into the Loop to sell."

"The Loop?" he replied in surprise. "You mean open up a store in downtown Chicago?"

"Well, not exactly," she explained. "But, look, don't you think people in Chicago would like my candy?"

"Like it? Of course they'd like it, Ora. But, well, I mean. *I* like your candy because *you* made it. Your friends like your candy because *you* make it. It's good candy. Fine candy, but . . . "

"But if you and our friends . . . "

"Now, now Ora. After all, I'm nearly well, and I'm back at my desk, and . . . "

"It isn't that, dear."

"No?"

"It's just that I believe in my candy, and I believe I can do a job selling it."

So Mrs. Snyder went into Chicago's Loop, to the proprietor of a coffee store and told him of the success of her candy in the school store and at church bazaars in Maywood. "I want to sell it here," she told the coffee-store manager, "on consignment. I'll make it, and you can give me a little space for it here, and I'll pay you a percentage on my sales."

"I'm afraid your enthusiasm has got the better of your good judgment, Mrs. Snyder," she was told. "Who'd buy home-made candy in a store? No, I'm afraid it wouldn't work out."

"But you could give it a trial. It's good candy and people say . . . "

"I know. I know. The folks at home like it. But here in the Loop."

"Look, I brought a box here with me. Try a piece, please."

"Sure. Thanks. I'll . . . m'mmmm. Say, that *is* divinity."

"Then you'll give it a trial?"

"M'mmm. Well. Yes. I'll give it a trial. But I warn you. People just won't spend their hard-earned money on candy they can make in their own kitchens!"

The little consignment candy business on State Street prospered. Soon it had outgrown its humble environs.

Ora Snyder grew with it, grew from the status of house-wife and mother to the status of a full-fledged business woman. Soon she opened a small shop on Dearborn; then another, and another, until there were fifteen in Chicago and suburbs, employing 225 persons and dispensing 300 different kinds of candy.

With success, representatives of a large corporation came to her with the proposition of opening stores in her name in every city in America. "We are authorized," they told her, "to offer you a substantial number of shares in the concern, and . . . a handsome salary besides."

But Mrs. Snyder told them, "I'm not interested." Pointing to the wall of her store, she continued, "There. That's my picture. I didn't put it there because I'm vain. I put it there because Mrs. Snyder is really in the candy business. I personally supervise every piece of candy that is sold in my shops. That name is not for sale. I worked hard to make that name mean something—good, whole-some, home-made candy—to my customers."

Mrs. Snyder is at her office every day, all day, and she personally originates and samples every batch of candy. The public, however, is not accustomed to that personal supervision, as this amusing anecdote indicates. Several years ago Mrs. Snyder had a sales girl with a lisp. A gentleman making a purchase asked the young lady if there was a real Mrs. Snyder. "Oh, yeth," said the girl.

The gentleman said in reply, "Oh, I thought she was only a myth."

And the lisping sales girl answered, "No, a mithuth!"

"Women may have the greatest sweet tooth," reports Mrs. Snyder out of her experience, "but men like candy just as well as women—perhaps a lot better. Twenty-nine years ago, when I started my business, it was considered effeminate for a man to admit openly that he liked candy. He was very timid in asking for a bag of candy for himself, which he stuck in his pocket to eat later in the solitude of his office. But today things are different. The same man buys candy not only for his family, but for himself and his office force as well. It was because I discovered man's great love of candy that I opened my first candy shop on Dearborn Street in the Loop, Dearborn Street being a typical man's street."

Besides the well-earned picture of herself in her stores, Mrs. Snyder has a total of 500 framed photographs of outstanding men and women whom she has met across the counter in her candy shops. Eddie Cantor, John T. McCutcheon, Fanny Brice, Ed Wynne, Helen Morgan, Mary Pickford and many, many others have been her customers.

"No success," says Mrs. Snyder, "can be attained without confidence in yourself, in your merchandise and in your public. On the other hand, over-optimism may be fatal. Never say 'Yes' today. It is much more important to know when to say 'No.' Sleep on all decisions. Listen carefully to advice but mind your own business. And remember, the product you are selling must be what you say it is and more. When you start with confidence, ambition and determination in yourself and in your merchandise, your success is assured. And, above all, keep happy. For happiness is like jam, you can't spread it, even a little without getting some on yourself. Personality is the greatest factor in business, and a smile is the greatest factor in personality. It takes only fourteen muscles to smile, while sixty-four muscles are used in a frown. Why work overtime on disagreeable business?"

Yes, twenty-nine years ago a woman made a batch of candy costing five cents. She used an egg and a cup of sugar Yes, and some other ingredients went into that candy, too. Hard work, determination in the face of adversity, the will to win. All these were part of the formula.

Today that same woman, wife, mother and grandmother, stood over another batch of candy. She tasted a piece and approved. That candy went to fifteen modern, up-to-date stores, to be sold to a waiting public that knows the merit of honesty, the quality behind the simple, unpretentious name on the front of the stores—MRS. SNYDER'S CANDIES!

Oh, whether it's business or whether it's sport,
    Study the rules.
Know every one of them, long and the short.
    Study the rules.
Know what you may do, and what you may not.
Know what your rights are. 'Twill help you a lot

In the critical times when the battle is hot.
  Study the rules.

Life's not a scramble, and sport's not a mess.
  Study the rules.
Nothing is left to haphazard or guess.
  Study the rules.
Know what's a foul blow, and what is a fair;
Know all the penalties recognized there;
Know what to go for, and what to beware.
  Study the rules.

Nature has fixed for us definite laws.
  Study the rules!
Every effect is the child of a cause.
  Study the rules.
Nature has penalties she will inflict,
When it comes to enforcing them nature is strict.
Her eyes are wide open. She never is tricked.
  Study the rules.

Play to your best in the game as it's played.
  Study the rules.
Know how a fair reputation is made.
  Study the rules.
Sport has a standard, and life has a plan—
Don't go at them blindly; learn all that you can—
Know all that is asked and required of a man.
  Study the rules!

—*Study the Rules*

WINDING THE CLOCK

When I was but a little lad, my old Grandfather said
That none should wind the clock but he, and so, at time
　　for bed,
He'd fumble for the curious key kept high upon the shelf
And set aside that little task entirely for himself.

In time Grandfather passed away, and so that duty fell
Unto my Father, who performed the weekly custom well;
He held that clocks were not to be by careless persons
　　wound,
And he alone should turn the key or move the hands
　　around.

I envied him that little task, and wished that I might be
The one to be entrusted with the turning of the key;
But year by year the clock was his exclusive bit of care
Until the day the angels came and smoothed his silver
　　hair.

To-day the task is mine to do, like those who've gone
　　before
I am a jealous guardian of that round and glassy door,
And 'til at my chamber door God's messenger shall knock
To me alone shall be reserved the right to wind the clock.

[182]

HARD LINES

A drawing board, paper, black ink and a brush—there you have "Dick Tracy," detective—hero of one of America's most popular cartoon strips, shown daily in more than two hundred newspapers. Of course, first you must have an idea, and you must have Chester Gould, for Mr. Gould is Dick Tracy's creator, inspiration and—literally—guiding hand.

Chester Gould's story is the story of a boy who wanted to become a cartoonist and did it, in spite of obstacle after obstacle. Chester Gould, originator of the famous crime fighter, began seeking his fortune in Chicago back in 1920. Chet Gould held job after job, six weeks for one, four weeks for another and all at a salary that barely provided a living. Dim indeed grew his hope for a career as a cartoonist. But he held on; he would not give up on a dream he had had as a boy back in Pawnee, Oklahoma in the year 1907.

Chet's father was a printer on the Courier Dispatch, and in the evening when he would come home he would be greeted by his son with the cry:

"Daddy! Daddy! Did you bring me home those . . . you know . . . those things that if you put a paper on 'em you can draw pictures? You know . . . "

"You mean, the matrices, son?" replied Mr. Gould. "Sure I brought 'em . . . a lot of them. Here they are."

"Gee . . . goody. They're swell. Thanks, Daddy."

"You're welcome, Chester," said Mr. Gould with a laugh. "From the looks of things now, you'll probably be a printer like me when you grow up. Eh, son?"

"Printer?" answered the boy uncertainly. "Well, no, Daddy. I . . . I don't want to be a printer. I'm going to be a . . . a drawer. I mean painter. Have you got an extra pencil, Dad?"

Another day it was to his mother that Chester appealed for aid.

"Mother . . . mother!"

"Yes, Chester."

"Mother, I hate to bother you when you're sewing, but gee . . . look at this, Mommie."

"The magazine, dear?"

"No, this advertisement. Listen . . . 'You, too, can be a successful cartoonist. Do as hundreds of others have done. Join our correspondence school and learn cartooning. Make big money.' And mother," he exulted, "it's only twenty dollars for the *whole* course."

"Only twenty dollars? Why, that's a great deal of money, Chester. Much more than your father and I can afford. But I think it would be splendid if you sent for the course . . . after you've *earned* the money."

The time came when Chester Gould *did* follow in the footsteps of his father . . . more or less. He became a cub reporter on the Daily Oklahoman, but his thoughts and dreams were more on cartoons than reporting.

"Gould! Gould! *Where* is that cub?" shouted Harrison, the boss. *"Gould!"*

[184]

"Yes, Mr. Harrison. Sorry I didn't hear you. You see, I got a new idea for a cartoon for the sports page tomorrow. You see, here's the . . . "

"Gould," interrupted Harrison, "I'm afraid you haven't quite got the idea of how the Daily Oklahoman is run and of *your* part in helping make it run. This is May 15, and we go to press pretty soon, and you get fifteen dollars a week as cub reporter, and . . . "

"I've been wanting to speak to you about that, Mr. Harrison," spoke up Chester. "You see, I feel that I ought to get paid something for my sport cartoons . . . "

"Ought to get *paid* for them?" exclaimed Harrison, surprised. "You ought to thank your lucky stars I let you draw them . . . and then thank me again for printing them without *charging* you for it. Why, of all the infernal nerve . . . "

"I'm sorry, Mr. Harrison," said Chester determinedly. "I guess we just don't see eye-to-eye on my cartoons. But I'm going to Chicago this Fall, and . . . and try . . . "

"*Try* is right," inserted the crusty newspaper man. "You'll be back here in Oklahoma City looking for your old job or my name isn't . . . "

"That's where you're wrong," predicted Chester. "Dead wrong. I won't be back . . . and I *will* be a cartoonist, and a *good* one, too."

But it wasn't as easy as young Gould may have anticipated at that moment. The years went by, and he became almost a joke in the Windy City peddling his cartoons. On the side he did commercial art at fifteen dollars a week when he wasn't being tossed about the various newspaper offices. "But I'll crack it yet," he promised himself and others. Every Monday morning he made his regular call at the Tribune Syndicate.

Rivals who knew about his persistent determination to make the Trib, said, "If he had half as much talent as he has persistence, the Trib would be *hounding* him . . . instead of the other way around."

But Chester was not only persistent; he was diligent, too. Night after night his pencil raced across the drawing board, creating, dreaming, creating. By day he worked for one paper or another, but each day, at noon, he took his last night's effort to the Century, fast train to New York, and sent his work speeding to the desk of the editor of the Tribune Syndicate, now located in New York City. And day after day he waited for the magic telegram which would inform him that at last his work had been accepted. The word, however, did not come, and almost in desperation he sought the counsel of a friend.

"After all, Chet, you're doing all right," he was told. "True, you're not making big money, and you aren't famous; but how many of us are?"

"It isn't that," replied Gould. "It's . . . it's just that I feel that fame, money, doing the thing you want to do . . . they're all possible, if a fellow can only think of a new twist, a new angle."

"Why don't you try bootlegging?" suggested his friend. "They say the rackets are where the big money is . . . in

[186]

The kitchen where the kettle sings
    The stairway where the children race
And all the long familiar things
    Which every nook and corner grace;
The street where neighbors come and go
    And pride and sham have ceased to be
The wall where climbing roses grow,
    All these and more are home to me.

The dining table set for four,
    The merry sound of spoon on plate,
The children clamoring for more
    With eyes aglow and hearts elate.
The hours when we can be alone
    From all the vain pretensions free
Where rest and peace and love are known,
    All these and more are home to me.

                   —Home

Bit of a priest and a bit of sailor,
Bit of a doctor and bit of a tailor,
Bit of a lawyer and bit of detective,
Bit of a judge, for his work is corrective;
Cheering the living and soothing the dying,
Risking all things, even dare-devil flying;
True to his paper and true to his clan—
Just look him over, the newspaper man.

Sleep! There are times that he'll do with a little,
Work till his nerves and his temper are brittle;

[189]

Fire cannot daunt him, nor long hours disturb him,
Gold cannot buy him and threats cannot curb him;
Highbrow or lowbrow, your own speech he'll hand you,
Talk as you will to him, he'll understand you;
He'll go wherever another man can—
That is the way of the newspaper man.

One night a week may he rest from his labor,
One night at home to be father and neighbor;
Just a few hours for his own bit of leisure,
All the rest's gazing at other men's pleasure,
All the rest's toiling, and yet he rejoices,
All the world is, and that men do, he voices—
Who knows a calling more glorious than
The day-by-day work of the newspaper man?

—The Newspaper Man

MEET THE CHAMP

"MEET the Champ!" That vital bit of American phraseology usually is followed by the appearance of a young, husky, bronzed American. But not always! Friends told Mark G. Harris that it was impossible to learn golf at sixty-six. Nevertheless, Mark Harris took up the game when he was that age, and at seventy-five years of age stands as America's greatest on the putting green.

A successful retired businessman seeking California's golden sunshine one day back in 1927, Mark Harris was sitting on the veranda of the Ambassador Hotel chatting with a group of friends from his home city, Chicago.

"Well, Mark," observed a friend, "how do you feel after a few days of our California sunshine?"

"Like sixteen, instead of sixty-six!" replied Harris.

"Better be careful, Mark. Don't get to feeling too good or you'll be wanting to get back into the harness again."

"Mark might want to," spoke up another friend present, "but orders are orders, particularly when they're doctor's orders. How about it, Mark?"

"That's right," answered Mark, "but that doesn't mean a fellow can't find *some* outlet for his energy."

At that moment the golf professional in charge of the eighteen-hole pitch-and-putt course at the hotel happened to pass by. "I guess I'll go down with him and have a look at it," spoke up Harris.

"Don't let him talk you into playing, Mark," cautioned his friends. "They don't allow beginners on the course here."

But after looking over the little course, Mark observed to the pro, "Say, that's really a layout, that little course. Why, a fellow'll get more sunshine there in a minute than . . . I believe I'll take up this game."

"Well," replied the pro skeptically. "Golf's a game a fellow's got to start working at when he's a youngster. You can't begin . . . "

"I say," replied Mark, "that if a man has a live spirit, a perseverance that never falters and the 'know-how' to do things right, he can do a lot of things called and thought impossible!"

And from that moment, the name of Mark G. Harris was ticketed to be added to the roster of champions of golf. Mr. Harris began his study of the "short game" of golf, the approach shots to the green and the science of putting. Day after day he perfected his strokes, pursued the knowledge of the professional. Then he returned to Chicago to seek out the tutelage of Bob MacDonald, who had been recommended to him as an outstanding teacher.

"So you want instruction, at your age?" MacDonald greeted him.

"My age? Why, I'm just a boy. I'm only sixty-six," came back Harris.

"Besides," demurred MacDonald, "I'm quite busy on my book. You see, I'm writing a book on golf instruction, and . . . "

"Good. Fine. With me as your pupil, you'll be able to write first-hand on my case. And I'm sure you'll find me an interesting pupil. You see, I have a theory that I can master the short game, really become expert at it."

"Well, I don't want to discourage you, Mr. Harris, but I'm afraid you're a little optimistic. You see, golf, good golf, takes years and years of hard work and . . . "

But Mark Harris' enthusiasm and sincerity won over the golf professional, and Mr. Harris continued his newly-found career. In 1931 he was back in Los Angeles. There, at the Rancho Golf Club a group of interested spectators were watching him in action before the movie cameras.

"So that's the seventy-year old wizard of the putter?" commented one of the bystanders.

"That's Mark Harris, all right," said another. "That is the 'short game' master just about to make a chip shot. Listen to the announcer."

"Ladies and gentlemen," came the announcement. "Mr. Harris is now going to attempt a mashie chip shot from thirty-five feet. He takes his stance, looks at the flag and swings. The ball hits the green. It's on a line with the hole. It's dribbling toward . . . it's in the hole! Ladies and gentlemen, Mark G. Harris holed his first shot. A mashie chip shot from thirty-five feet. In one!"

That day, the motion picture cameras recorded one of the greatest sports phenomena of today, or any other day. Mark Harris accomplished the impossible, piling on one unbelievable shot after another. And he has continued to do the unbelievable ever since.

Last year, his book, *Putting Made Easy* was published by Reilly and Lee of Chicago, and golfers everywhere acclaimed it as a real contribution to the literature of golf. This year he designed a new putter, known as the Mark G. Harris perfect balance putter, against the beliefs of many noted designing authorities, and that putter is being purchased by golfers everywhere in America.

The reason there is only about one good golfer among every five thousand of the two million persons playing the game in the United States is, according to Mark Harris, that "many people have an inferiority putting complex, and that naturally is a big handicap. How can a man become a good putter? By disbelieving that a person must be born a good putter. Besides this, very few players have any putting system or methodical method of playing this shot. Putting looks easy, but it is the hardest stroke in the bag to conquer for the following reasons: In making a drive if the player lands on the fairway which is generally from 150 to 200 feet wide, he is O.K. for his next shot; but when he is on the green and making his putting shot, he is shooting at a cup which is only four and one-quarter inches in diameter, and he has to contend with slopes, hollows and pebbles on the green."

Yet Mr. Harris, starting in at the age of sixty-six, has proved that this most difficult of all the difficult feats of golf can be conquered by intelligent and persistent effort.

The eighteenth hole and the evening gloam,
The end is near and I'm getting home!
The club house looms in the twilight shade,
Where the boys will ask me with whom I played,
And just what sort of a score I made.

It's the eighteenth hole and the game is done;
What matters it now have I lost or won?
In many a pit and trap I've been,
I've had the thrill of a contest keen,
But I'm coming home with my record clean.

The best and the worst of the sport I've had—
Some shots were good and a few were bad.
I made mistakes which I couldn't mend,
I've lost many a hole but never a friend,
And now I've come where the fairways end.

Lord, when I come to the eighteenth hole
And my last putt drops, as I homeward stroll,
May I be met at the club house door
By the boys who have all holed out before,
And be welcomed there though I failed to score!

—The Eighteenth Hole

FISHING

My grandfather said with a toss of his head,
  As he sat at the fire making flies,
Tying silk upon hooks for his old leather books
  And being mighty proud of his ties:
"Oh, the sport is a joy! But remember, my boy,
  Only hungry men work for the dish.
The creel's but a part of this glorious art;
  There is much more to fishing than fish.

"From spring unto fall I can answer the call
  To go out on my favorite streams,
And when wintry winds bite I can sit here at night,
  Enjoying my fancies and dreams.
For the soul can be stirred, both by blossom and bird,
  And the wonders that lie all about.
There are volumes of lore it's a joy to explore;
  Oh, there's much more to fishing than trout.

"It's not all in the catch; there's a thrill in the hatch,
  And knowing the birds by their song.
There's the tying of hooks and the reading of books,
  Which last a man all his life long;
Not a fisherman he who contented can be
  With the whirr of the reel and the swish
Of a taut running line, for the art is too fine!
  There is much more to fishing than fish."

STAGE MONEY

THERE was no crying on the other fellow's shoulder for Charles Darrow, the world's greatest maker and breaker of millionaires. Darrow is the man who can run you up into the millions and then let you down with a thud. He is the inventor of the game, MONOPOLY, one of America's recent game crazes.

One evening late in November of the year 1933 the company Charles Brace Darrow was working for folded up. But when Darrow came home with the news to his lovely wife that evening, he simply said, "Now, there's no use getting all excited. What's happened has happened, and there's nothing we can do about it. I'll rest a day or two and then start the hunt for another."

"Of course you'll find something," she encouraged him. "Architects are always in demand."

But that new job wasn't as easy to find as Darrow expected. He walked into and out of more business offices than he thought existed, but always the answer was the same: "Sorry, Mr. Darrow, you're a good man, but we just haven't an opening."

After ten months, Mr. Darrow found his bank account flat. Something had to be done. Mowing lawns helped pay grocery bills; building odd pieces of furniture in the basement workshop helped with the rent. And then while reading the evening paper, Charlie Darrow found an interesting news item.

"Listen, Nell," he observed. "Here's a smart idea. 'Princeton professor uses stage money in classroom transactions. Students make a game of trading in real estate and market operations.' Not bad, eh, Nell?"

"Quite interesting," replied Nell.

"You know, Nell," Charlie continued, "I'm going to make some stage money just so you and I won't forget how it feels to handle a dollar bill."

"Goodness knows, it's been a long time since we handled any bills, except the grocery and rent bills."

"Don't worry, dear," he promised. "It won't be long now. I'm going to crack something right soon."

And Charles Darrow set to work to make stage money just for the fun of it. With a fist full of this stage money, he began to make imaginary speculations. Then one evening some friends, the Jamesons, came over for a visit, and Nell suggested, "Why not make a game of this stage money buying and we'll all play."

"Not bad, my dear, not half bad," agreed Darrow. "I'll draw up some charts, and make some more stage money, and we'll have some fun."

The Jamesons came over, and Charles and Nell introduced them to a game. The Jamesons took to Charlie's game, took to it as hundreds of thousands were to take to it later. When Charlie Darrow awoke the next morning, he found his wife carefully paging through the classified pages of the Philadelphia telephone directory.

"Good morning, dear," he greeted her. "Interesting reading I imagine."

"I'm finding it so at the moment," she replied.

"If you come across anything of special interest, read it out loud. I don't want to miss anything."

"Don't worry, you're not going to miss a thing. Listen: Parker Game Company, 1341 Spruce Street."

"Parker Game Company?" he demanded. "Say, what is this?"

"I hope a fortune," she told him. "Anyway, you're going visiting this morning, and the address is the one I've just read—1341 Spruce Street. It's the address of the Parker Game Company, one of the best in the business."

At the address on Spruce Street Mr. Parker told them, "I never like to be over-encouraging, Mr. Darrow, for it too often leads to disappointment. But in this new game, I honestly believe you have a winner."

"I hope you're even half right, Mr. Parker."

"Well, we'll see. The Parker Company is going to manufacture and market your game, and we're going to call it—MONOPOLY. Mr. Darrow, the Parker Game Company has always believed that its business, the business of building and creating games, is a most important one for it brings joy and pleasure to the family circle, and in these days that is important."

Mr. Darrow, America's living room financier, says that he probably would not have come upon Monopoly if he had not been unemployed. "You see," he adds, "games have always appealed to me. I'm just a boy at heart. I have always liked thinking of new things to accomplish, but I like to have fun in doing them."[2]

[199]

Keep your dreams—they're richer far
Than the facts discovered are.

Do not seek all things to touch;
Do not want to know too much.

Growing old, still play the child;
Keep some glory undefiled.

What if clouds are mist and air?
Still see ships sailing there.

What would life be if we knew
Only those things which are true?

If the things of bad and good
Were by all men understood,

Nature's hills and brooks and springs
Would be catalogued as things.

Keep your dreams, for in them lies
Joy denied to men grown wise.

Still build castles in the air!
Still see white ships sailing there!

Still have something to pursue
Something which you wish you knew.
                    —*Keep Your Dreams*

LIE DETECTIVE

PROFESSOR LEONARDE KEELER of the Scientific Crime Detection Laboratory of the Northwestern University School of Law at Evanston, Illinois, believed that he could build a machine that would record human emotions, a machine that when used on a human being would detect a lie. As a result of his determination to succeed in the face of adverse public opinion, his name, together with such great ones as Professor Hugo Munsterberg, Dr. William Marsten, Benussi, Burt and Crossland, is indelibly written in the annals of modern crime detection methods.

It was as an eager boy of fourteen watching a policeman, John Larsen, at work in the Berkeley, California police station, that Keeler became infatuated with the idea of perfecting a "lie detector." Chief August Vollmer, who was for twenty-five years chief of the Berkeley Police Department and is now a professor at the University of California, had assigned Patrolman Larsen to the task of developing the lie-detector. Vollmer had read of the work being done at Harvard by Munsterberg and Marsten and was determined to investigate its possibilities. Young Keeler followed Chief Vollmer to Los Angeles where he spent a year working on the polygraph. Then he enrolled at Leland-Stanford University, majoring in psychology.

Upon graduation he secured employment in the State of Illinois criminologist's office at Joliet Penitentiary, where he continued his work on the polygraph. Then, in 1930, he was appointed to the staff of the Northwestern University Scientific Crime Detection Laboratory, where he continued his experiments.

Meanwhile, the attitude of the public had begun to change. The much-maligned "lie-detector," hitherto a Sunday supplement subject of great conjecture, had been employed in securing evidence with telling effect. The bar, the bench, the police—even the criminal element— had developed a healthy respect for the instrument designed by Professor Keeler.

Today, in the Northwestern Laboratory, over a thousand persons a year submit themselves to examination by the lie-detector. And today, Leonarde Keeler, the boy who believed such a machine could be built, sits in that laboratory, working, working, to the end that scientific crime detection should be available to police authorities everywhere.

"Many of the subjects we examine," Professor Keeler explains, "are members of bank personnels, department stores and other commercial institutions. We examine applicants for positions in some twenty business institutions before they are hired.

"We fasten a cuff around the person's arm to get his blood pressure and pulse, and place a tube around his chest so that we can record his breathing. Then we fasten a clip around his hand so as to get the activity of the sweat glands.

"Then we ask him some questions. The operator plays

upon the emotions of the subject. Through this questioning he builds up tension to a certain given point and then under other circumstances produces relief. The instrument records many of the bodily changes which accompany emotions, such as: blood pressure, pulse, breathing and the activity of the sweat glands in the hand. Almost all individuals who are subjected to the test are naturally nervous, but no matter how nervous or how calm, almost all individuals will show greatest emotional tension at one point if guilty and at another point if innocent."

The system that the present lie-detector is based on was used as far back as 1500 when Benvenuto Cellini, the famous sculptor and goldsmith, was caught by his father through taking his pulse. Thence it passed on down through the years to the present time when, through the aid of scientific and electric equipment, it has been perfected. The achievement has proved a great aid of law enforcement agencies the country over, and test results have been admitted as evidence in the Court of Law, though Professor Keeler will not allow them to be introduced as evidence except in cases where the defense and the prosecutor have stipulated in advance that the tests shall be so admitted.

> The night school swings its doors for all;
>   Near-by the libraries are.
> Who will, has knowledge at his call,
>   Nor need he travel far.
> Not much for wisdom need he pay,

However poor the lad,
He has a better chance today
Than Lincoln ever had.

However lowly born he seems,
A richer child is he
Than Lincoln, with his youthful dreams,
Who read beneath a tree.
However poor the circumstance
Which hedges him around,
Life offers him a better chance
Than Abraham Lincoln found.

Oh, boy, if courage you possess,
And have the will to learn,
No one can keep you from success,
From book to book you'll turn.
No library shelf to you is barred,
No school denied to you,
Your battle cannot be as hard
As that which Lincoln knew.

Who has the will to understand.
Will find wise teachers near;
The poorest urchin in the land
Has but himself to fear,
For 'spite of humble circumstance
And fate and fortune sad,
To-day gives boys a better chance
Than Lincoln ever had.

—Every Boy's Chance